NOR
W

Buying a Bargain Car
at Auction

Buying a Bargain Car at Auction

RUPERT STOCK

ROBERT HALE · LONDON

Robert Hale Limited
Clerkenwell House
Clerkenwell Green
London EC1R 0HT

Photoset in Times Roman by
Derek Doyle & Associates, Mold, Clwyd.
Printed in Great Britain by
St Edmundsbury Press Ltd, Bury St Edmunds, Suffolk.
Bound by Hunter & Foulis

Contents

To Christine,
without whom there would be nothing,
for she is everything

Introduction

To the majority of private individuals buying a car, the world of car auctions is a mystery. Moreover, from the fleeting glimpses of it seen on television, or in the press, the whole setting seems awesome and accordingly best avoided despite the tempting reports of some of the bargains obtained.

This book has been written, therefore, to explain all the mysteries and remove the fears. Every step of the process of buying at auction is described in detail so that, armed with the knowledge gained from this book, the buyer can make his purchase confident in the knowledge that he has bought his car at a competitive price and with the minimum of risk.

For stylistic reasons and ease of reference I have adopted 'he' and 'him' throughout rather than the clumsy 'he or she', 'him or her' and would apologize to anyone offended as a result.

Acknowledgements

My thanks to Betty Kemp who so bravely toiled to decipher my terrible handwriting and without whose help this book would still be the ungainly pile of scribblings that represented a favour I had no right to ask.

Thanks also go to John Hale for his interest, advice and infinite patience in steering me through the unknown world of publishing.

1 The Reason for Buying a Car at Auction

Recession or not, the UK new car market largely holds its own with registration varying between 1½ and 2 million a year. These figures clearly indicate that a substantial proportion of car owners never consider buying a second-hand vehicle. What is less clear is the reason why people continue to throw money at such an expensive and rapidly depreciating luxury when, with reasonable care and enterprise, a nearly-new or used car can be bought for thousands of pounds less than retail price with virtually no risk.

During its first six months, the average new car loses some 25% to 30% of its list price. Moreover, the larger part of the depreciation occurs the moment the car leaves the showroom. For example in April 1994 a new L-registration Ford Mondeo 1.8LX 5-door had a list price of £12,725, yet a five-month-old model with the same specifications and which had covered only 6,000 miles sold for £9,500 at auction. Also, as the following graph shows, the rate of depreciation of a car can be expected to slow down dramatically after the first six months of its life.

Whilst one cannot dispute the prestige value in a new car, it must be doubted whether many buyers, particularly those of popular models, realize what a high price they are paying for that prestige. As for reliability, how much is one sacrificing by buying a vehicle which has a properly recorded full service history, or indeed one which has only covered, say, 6,000 miles? In the latter case it is more than likely that

Graph to Show Decrease in Value of a Typical Family Car against Increase in Age

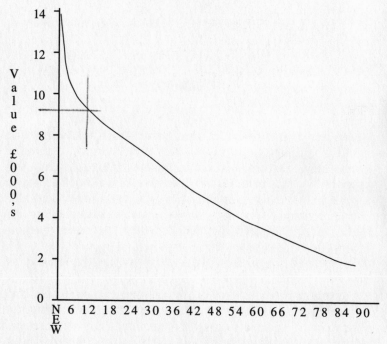

Age of Car (months) from New

Drawn from figures showing typical depreciation of a £13,850 car between 1987 and 1994 courtesy of Glass's Guide Services Ltd. (Depreciation calculated from trade values on ten models over the period and an average taken to create a hypothetical £13,850 car) the manufacturer's warranty is still operative and that any teething troubles have been resolved.

Undoubtedly some potential buyers are apprehensive in principle about buying a car off the forecourt, despite the fact that the majority of traders are honest. Nevertheless, even the honest garage has to pay for its expensive premises and make a profit. Consequently this book seeks to show how the private individual can buy his car at the price the dealer pays, with little or no risk and probably cheaper financing should that be required. With the second-hand car market structured as it is today, the private buyer's best option must be to buy at an auction, particularly if he focuses on a well-serviced or low mileage ex-fleet car.

Auctions are, in effect, the wholesale division of the used-car market and it is their involvement with the all-powerful company car fleets which gives them this position. To put the buying power of UK car fleets into perspective, one only needs to consider that of the total 1993 sales of Vauxhall Cavaliers approximately 75% went to the fleet market. And of all Ford car sales in this country about 50% were to fleets.

These fleet vehicles are almost entirely disposed of through auctions, with sales to staff and trade representing only a fraction of the total. Often the larger companies, and especially those with high public profile, have an auction-only policy to avoid accusations of preferential selling. For them, auctions offer a clean, effective and quick method of selling cars at a fair market value and without hassle. Auctions have therefore become a market-place in themselves where the trade price of all used cars is determined.

The following examples of April 1994 prices show the difference between trade ('wholesale') and retail prices:

Mondeo 93L 1.8LX 5DR	Auction: £9,500 (6,000 miles)
	Retail: £11,200 (8,450 miles)
Cavalier 90G 1.8L 5DR	Auction: £3,200 (80,000 miles)
	Retail: £4,995 (61,000 miles)
Cavalier 2.0GL 4DR	Auction: £3,925 (90G 60,000 miles)
	Retail: £4,695 (89F 56,000 miles)

Fiesta 1.1 Popular Plus 3DR 1. Auction: £2,850 (89G 38,000 miles)
Retail: £3,995 (89G 39,000 miles)
2. Auction: £3,150 (90G 24,000 miles)
Retail: £4,295 (90G 20,000 miles)

This difference exists, of course, regardless of model, date etc.

Looking at these figures it is immediately apparent that the fleet companies are putting nearly-new and used cars into auctions throughout the country at prices which, for the private buyer, are at bargain level. The reason for this lies in the structure of the second-hand car market as a whole and the auction in particular.

Although the auction is primarily fleet orientated, it also sells on behalf of main dealers, traders, major chains of garages and, to a lesser extent, private individuals. The auction relies on all these categories, not so much for what they are selling but for their buying power. The fleet entry on which the sales flourishes is dependent upon the traders who currently buy the majority of cars and without whom the quick hassle-free disposal element of the sale would be lost. Disposal is the word used by these firms, and speed, not so much price, is the essence.

Nearly-new cars tend to sell to main agents whereas direct ex-fleet vehicles three or more years old go to larger traders and garages, leaving much of the rest to small concerns. Throughout the wide spectrum of buyers there is a common factor. By buying a used car at an auction, valeting it and offering it to the public at a considerable mark-up, the trader shows a profit even if he operates from an expensive showroom.

But how can the fleet owner, however large, afford to take such huge and apparently unnecessary losses in the first six months of ownership by buying new cars? Ford, Vauxhall, Rover, Renault and Citroen – top five manufacturers in terms of UK sales – sell to the larger fleets at amazing discounts, hoping thereby to improve and maintain their position in the league table by registering the maximum number of cars sold each year. It is rumoured that one of the high street banks has managed to secure discounts even greater than those granted to main dealers and perhaps as much as 40% off the list price. That same company is currently selling many of its cars when they are only four months old and reputedly making a profit. Certainly discounts of 30% to major players are not unheard of. With, for example, 75% of Vauxhall Cavaliers going to the fleet market at a high discount, it is little wonder that a nearly-new car is obtainable at such a bargain price at auction.

Whilst price is therefore the major advantage for the private buyer at auction, there are other benefits which should be considered.

Why Buy at Auction?

1) The cars are sold for considerably less than retail.
2) There is plenty of time to inspect the car's bodywork before the sale.
3) Whilst carrying out your preliminary inspection and throughout the transaction you will not be hassled by overpowering salespeople.
4) All mileages are declared as being correct or incorrect, leaving no room for doubt, and providing an avenue for recourse where mileages declared correct are proved to be false. Many forecourts issue disclaimers on all mileages, leaving doubts in the mind and by their nature providing no security. At auction the buyer knows where he stands.
5) Every car sold through auction attracts an indemnity fee. This fee represents an 'insurance' against three key elements:
a) Total loss. This is usually defined as being registered on HPI's VCAR or Vehicle Condition Alert Registers (see Chapter 8).
b) Theft or Security alert. You are guaranteed clear title to the car.
c) Outstanding Hire Purchase. Responsibility for payment of finance agreements in the form of hire purchase secured on any one vehicle passes with ownership of that vehicle. (You may have struck a very good deal for cash with a private or even 'semi-trade' figure only to have your newly

acquired car repossessed by a firm with whom you have never even dealt (see Chapter 8).

6) Finance agreements can readily be taken out on cars bought at auction where the finance house with whom you have struck a deal pays the auctioneers direct. Needless to say, this entails a little more work on your part than would setting up finance at the forecourt, but remember that by this method you will be free to shop around for the best contract and you will not be party to the 'kick back' or commission that the finance houses give to the dealers for getting you signed up. This commission is indeed a hefty amount in some cases and I know of some dealers who offer their cars for sale at remarkable discounts but insist that the buyer take out finance when they do so. Their reasoning is clear: reduce your profit margin on the point of sale but make up for it in finance commission.

Where commission is paid it must be recovered. The finance company often recovers it through having secured your business. Try going to the company you most favour direct and see which deal is ultimately the cheaper (see Chapter 6).

7) Payment. Auctions advertise themselves as being cash sales. This need not be taken quite so literally, as most, if not all, major auction houses will take cash, building society cheques or bankers drafts. The term 'Cash Sale Only' simply means that you will not be able to present a personal cheque over any amount guaranteed by your particular guarantee card. Remember all cheques, drafts etc. must be made payable to the auction company in question (see Chapter 5).

8) Mechanical Warranty is not available at auction, but cash savings are. Keep the money you save as your own 'warranty fund'. If warranty stands between you and the savings available at auction then there are three things to remember.

a) The dealer offering the warranty has actually bought that warranty on your behalf from an independent firm, much like buying life assurance. You will therefore be paying for the cover in the price of the car.

b) Because you are buying 'insurance' from an independent firm any claim you may have will be between you and the firm supplying it. The dealer will not be able to help.

c) We all know that every car has a limited lifespan, and as such these warranties are all very specific as to the extent and circumstances of the cover they provide. You will *definitely* need to *read the small print*. Remember, the dealer has probably bought his car at auction, may have blanket authority to register any vehicle under a certain age for warranty cover with his particular firm, and thus cannot give any guarantee that just because any one car has a warranty it will be any more reliable than the next of the same age.

9) Another problem often raised by the private buyer at auction is that of test drives. Unless you have bid on a car 'sold with warranty' or 'after sale test drive' you will not have the chance to test drive any car bought under the hammer (see Chapter 4 for details of 'warranty' at auction). Test drives, however, are not always that revealing. After all, a gearbox half full of sawdust can feel as smooth as silk for a few miles, and an egg mixed with powdered mustard slipped into the radiator will seal leaks well enough to get an HGV some 100 miles – even with a cracked cylinder head. Not to mention dry cement carefully spooned into a spinning flywheel to prevent clutch slip – a method that I employed as a student for eight months on my old Alfa Romeo before it finally failed its M.O.T. and was scrapped. Nevertheless, there is a way in which you might easily manage to achieve a test drive after the sale if you are confident of your ability to make the most of one (see Chapter 12).

With all the horror stories about test drives fresh in your mind, do not forget what it is that you are out to buy: a straight off the road, ex-fleet, well serviced car. Keep this in perspective by asking yourself *is* it likely that a major UK company would risk its good name (which will ultimately appear alongside your own in the log book), by selling onto the market cars that have had their mechanical condition disguised or doctored? I have never come across such a case. The only problems that crop up are due to wear and tear. This guide is designed to help you avoid these problems by picking the right lot, and by showing how to make the best of the time you have available to spot the defects. At the end of the day you will still have the money you saved by buying at auction to put right any problems that may emerge if you are unlucky.

10) The final outstanding advantage of buying at auction is that if, in the final analysis, you realize that you really don't like what you have bought – be it because it has turned out to be a horrible wreck or because you can't fit the bikes on the roof – then you still have the option open to you which is not available to anybody who has bought by any other method. *Sell it*, either through the auction from which it came (the best bet if you feel that you have been hard done by) or privately. I remember a young woman returning to one of my sales distraught at having spent the princely sum of £180 on her first car earlier in the day, only to find that it didn't drive as well as her Dad's company car. I offered the only solution that I could and, on taking my advice, she sold it in the night sale at a profit (see Chapter 14). Because you buy at wholesale prices there is an excellent chance of being able to re-sell at the same, if not slightly higher, price – especially if you are willing to put in an afternoon's polishing, hoovering and sprucing up. There are trade elements who make a living by doing only that. Had you bought at retail, then your risk of making a loss on selling is obviously considerably higher.

The auction environment is a better place for prospective buyers to make important decisions about valuation, condition, desirability and all the things we like to mull over before taking the decision to spend large sums of money.

The image of the auction as being fast-paced, with an air of rush and expectancy, is largely overblown. It is easy to forget that the sale itself, which is the moment that generates these feelings, represents only a small part of the company's week, albeit an important part. Few auction houses have a period of viewing of less than two hours before the sale starts, and the sale itself might last up to five hours. Thus you may find that the cars in which you are interested might be available for up to seven hours of inspection time – time in which to meticulously follow the guidelines in this and other specialized books listed in the bibliography.

The quality of this time is far greater than that available at a forecourt, or front drive of a vendor's house, for two important reasons:

1) You will not be hassled by a salesperson, as we have said before.

2) The car is presented in good light – dictated by the professionals who frequent the sale – and in the case of the 'Direct Company Car' is usually displayed in its off-the-road condition. Some auction houses carry out minor bodywork and paint repairs as part of their service to the fleet, and many fleet clients are insisting that their cars receive a good valet before the sale. Even so, it is not difficult to pick out a well looked after 'genuine' car when it is presented in its original state at the auction (see Chapters 9 & 10).

This book is designed and written to help you, the reader, understand what goes on at car auctions across the country and to dispel the fear of the business as a whole that has been instilled in the private individual. In America auctions are not nearly so accessible to the private buyer, with many sales closed to all but bona-fide car traders. Here there are few such restrictions, so *make the most of the opportunity* and use the information in this book to get the best out of our auction business.

Advantages and Disadvantages of Buying a Car at Auction

Of course the overriding advantage of buying a used car at auction is in the huge saving that is made. The prospective purchaser should be paying up to 25% less than he would for the same car at the garage forecourt. This may sound rash, but the sense of it all is only obvious when one realizes just where the bulk of these vehicles have come from.

Traders buy and sell at auction for a number of reasons, but primarily auctions exist to cope with the need for prime position garage space to be filled with stock at every moment of the selling day. Overheads are constant and without stock garagists cannot earn, and they can only earn by imposing mark-up on what they have bought. But how much mark-up can one afford to charge? This is the point at which every car pitch varies. Some put on a huge percentage and offer seemingly wonderful deals on part exchange; others deal in minimal margins and, in the extreme, may accept finance deals to cover only the cost of the cars – deals on which the finance company with whom you have signed up pay a healthy sum to the garagist in the form of commission.

But be it finance commission or wonderful deals on your old car, that garagist has as often as not sourced his stock from auction and has earned money out of *you*. What does he do with his part exchanges? Unless he can 'retail' his way out of the car for the money he gave you for it, he will offer it at auction at its real worth, perhaps four or five hundred pounds less than he paid you for it. This apparent loss to the dealer is of course balanced by the enormous gain that he achieved from you. Thus a part-exchange vehicle can often be negotiated to a lower price from the forecourt, because the dealer has a cushion from the original deal and will settle for anything more than the auction or 'trade' price that he knows the car could finally return to him.

What is it that makes such a long-standing and reputable business – that of selling cars from the forecourt – survive? The answer is warranty – something that your garagist will offer but the auctions do not. This, apart from good valet, is the only difference to you. In my opinion warranty from your garage is all you get when you pay that extra money; it is all that the salesmen can really 'sell'. At this point you have to study the warranty deal that you are being offered very, very carefully. Is it really as sound as it seems? After all, a warranty is simply an insurance policy taken out for yourself (again, you are paying) by the dealer, and you must remember that you are *both* bound by it. It isn't the dealer that will fix your car (should it go wrong) but the warranty firm, and this is why you must make sure that everything is properly covered. All too many of these warranties have clauses and provisos that make them worthless just when you need them most, and for good reason. After all, the warranty firm has to make a profit too, and we all know that every car has a limited life span.

The only other clause under which you are at risk when buying at auction is based on the fact that the vendors who sell through auction are not covered by some sections of the 'Sale of Goods' Act 1977/9 and are thus not liable to provide 'goods fit for any particular purpose', i.e. they sell 'as seen' (see Appendix 7). This act, though, should only be used in extreme cases anyway – and really, you have to ask yourself how much can go wrong? How much can it cost to put a car right and how much hassle do I need? After all, you will still have hold of that roughly 25% savings (typically £1,000) which will go a long way towards any problem you may or may not have!

It may sound risky, but with this book and your common sense you can reduce that risk, as can your choice of auction company. Two things are certain when buying at a reputable auction. Your indemnity fee of typically less than £100 provides that:

1) You will have full title to the car you buy and will not be liable for any hire purchase (HP) outstanding.

2) You will have been told whether the car has ever been an insurance total loss, i.e. ever sustained damage to a cost of repair representing say 50% or more of the value of the vehicle at the time of the accident.

HP and total loss and their consequences are a topic in themselves, but suffice it to say for now that HP may represent more than you paid for a car and is transferable with the vehicle, whilst a total loss vehicle carries, typically, half the value of its original equivalent.

2   Auction Procedure

Vehicle Entry

THE ENTRY FORM
To the auctioneers there are basically three types of car entry:
a) privately owned and entered;
b) trade entry;
c) direct fleet entry.

Whatever the source of the vehicle, the first stage is for an entry form to be drawn up. Different auctioneers have different types of entry forms. Happily, a type that is becoming increasingly popular is one that provides a top copy giving detailed information as to the make, model, mileage, and year of the car, all of which are crucial to its value. This top copy is often made available with the lot number stuck inside the windscreen of the car. If it is not there the auctioneer will read off the entry form all the necessary information at the time of offering the car for sale.

The entry form, in whatever guise, is a legal document. It may be referred to by Trading Standards officers at any time in the future and is admissible in court as evidence should it be required. Thus it is imperative that it should be drawn up correctly by whoever is entering the car. This is why entries received in categories (a) and nearly always (b) above are written by the vendor prior to sale and accepted over the counter by the auctioneers with the necessary documentation. This comprises the entry which should not be altered or added to by anybody but the vendor himself. The auction staff may ask a vendor to make alterations in order that the entry complies fully with their conditions.

Because of the need for the vendor to be responsible for the document for which the vehicle will be sold, the auctioneers are understandably reluctant to draw up the form or make any alteration to it on behalf of the vendor. In the case of category (c), direct fleet entry, there is little opportunity for the vendor himself to take the details needed from the car since he has probably not seen it for years, if at all!

Auctioneers collect on behalf of their fleet vendors from all over the country and, having returned the car to their nearest auction centre, they are compelled to draw up all the relevant information themselves, relying upon the company concerned for nothing more than declaration of the correct mileage, reserve and of total loss if applicable.

Fleet Log Books

Owing to the nature of the fleet entry it is very common for the car to be sold before the auctioneer has sight of the vehicle registration documents – simply because the car itself has been collected from its driver whose head office has all the documentation elsewhere. This being the case, the documents are said to be 'to follow' and should be declared so upon the entry form. Upon receipt they will be sent by the auctioneer to the purchaser. It is usually only when these documents have been received that the auctioneer will release payment of the funds from the sale of the vehicle to the vendor himself. This ensures that the documents arrive promptly and guards the auctioneer against there being any dispute over the description of or title to the car.

In the meantime it is possible for the purchaser to apply for his own documents in order that he may tax the vehicle. This can be done on the spot at the post office upon producing the auction receipt (ask for Form V62). Should you apply for your own log book still insist that the original be sent from the vendor, thus tying up the deal neatly.

The fact that direct fleet entries are drawn up in the office by auction staff, or even on the computer, means that it is easy where the top copies are displayed to discern between fleet, private and trade entry, which may be a great influence over your final choice of vehicle from the sale.

Look for neat handwriting, methodical completion without mistakes, little mention of fitted extras, official stamps and, most importantly, the words 'DIRECT FROM'.

End of Sale Trial

At the point of entry the decision is made by the vendor as to whether the vehicle should be sold with 'a trial' or 'with warranty'. This decision is either displayed on the top copy or announced at the point of sale and should also make up an important part of your choice.

Your choice of car may err towards a vehicle offered with a trial or 'warranty', but remember that because the company fleet operator does not draw up the entry form himself he frequently deems it as not being worth the hassle to offer his vehicles with any warranty at all. In some cases the company will not even warrant or guarantee the mileage as being correct, even when they may know that it is. All this stems from the fact that the employees of the usually large company concerned are aware of the weighty implications over warranted mileage and do not need the hassle. The result of this is to put the prospective purchaser of a fleet car off those not sold with a trial when in fact these well serviced, straight-off-the-road cars are probably the best in the entire auction! On the other side of the coin the trade or private entry cars offered without trial will probably be offered so for a reason.

For these and many other reasons your choice of car obviously relies on distinguishing its source. This is why you should understand in detail how the vehicle entry procedure operates. (This procedure will be referred to again in Chapter 9).

Reserves

At the bottom of the entry form is the prompt for a reserve price. Most car auction houses will allow the setting of reserves on any car less than ten years old or thereabouts, and it is rare that vehicles are sold without reserve. The ten-year rule is often waived in the case of vintage or collectors' vehicles with the result that the only 'No Reserve' sales are usually the real 'bangers'. The reserve is, therefore, a necessary evil and has an interesting effect on the sale of the vehicle in question.

Come what may, the auctioneer cannot sell any vehicle for less than reserve price without the vendor's consent. It is as often as not the vendor's ability to set a sensible reserve that controls the success of the sale as a whole. Furthermore, it is the vendor's ability to set a sensible reserve and have trust in the auctioneer to do his best job that returns him the best money for his car.

Surprisingly, putting a car 'on sale' during the auction, i.e. by announcing that the next highest bidder will buy the car outright, may actually rekindle interest which is strong enough to make bidding continue up £200 or so. For example, I recall a dreadful old Sierra from a major finance company that I valued at £350. To my horror, the reserve was set at £600. For three weeks we could get no better bid than £275, and before long the traders would not bother with it at all. I spoke to the vendor before the next auction and explained that a car put 'on sale' would draw more money. Unconvinced, they nevertheless dropped the reserve to £200. After struggling to reach the magic figure the auctioneer announced the car as being 'on sale'. Immediately everybody woke up and it sold for £350! Had the vendor set that reserve originally it might have fetched another £50 to £100 on the strength of being a 'fresh' saleable entry.

When dealing with a good auctioneer there is a fine line between setting a reserve and killing a sale. In the best scenario the auctioneer should be trusted to do his job to the best of the market's ability and sell or not at his discretion.

One last thing about a reserve. Don't be inclined to ask what it is unless you are thick-skinned. Auctioneers will rarely tell you the reserve on any vehicle, especially those that have not previously been offered. If you intend asking about reserve prices, it is safer to do so after the sale, or in the case of unsold cars well before they go through again!

Lotting Up

Once the majority of the vehicles to be offered have been entered, they should be lotted up or arranged into the order in which they will arrive in front of the rostrum to be sold. This procedure is an important one and carries the most productive of the auctioneer's few chances to affect the way in which his sale will run.

There are periods in any sale that are flat whilst others are buoyant, and as a general rule it is important to keep the bidders busy and create a 'buzz'. No trader feels comfortable bidding on a car that nobody else bids on, since it seems apparent that he must be bidding too much! It is the auctioneer's job to make the sale buzz, and this is only possible when cars are selling and people think they're missing out.

To this end, help is at hand through careful and selective lotting up. The sale must start with a bang. This means the first six or seven cars should be selected so as to be as saleable as possible, i.e. the reserve should be close to, or even less than, the actual value of the car. This explains why an experienced manager or auctioneer should do the lotting up.

After this burst of activity, saleable cars must be interspersed with those with higher reserves in a sensible pattern, whilst there should be a sprinkling reserved for, say, the second hour of the sale when the bidders are beginning to drift, both mentally and physically! The auctioneers will always keep back a few desirable vehicles until last in order to keep buyers at the sale until the bitter end. This stimulates a little helpful impulse buying.

Another useful psychological trick is to offer the nicer of two identical cars first, in order to set a precedent in everybody's mind as to the strong value of the model. Similarly, that with the lower mileage should appear first. Thus if one has a very heavily reserved Escort, say, a year older than the one with a sensible reserve, offer the older car first to make the new one seem 'cheap' by comparison.

It is difficult not to be drawn in by these psychological ploys, but it is worthwhile being aware of it. It should not worry prospective bidders over much, since we all fall for it throughout our buying lives, probably nowhere more so than during our trips to the supermarket every week!

What one does need to be wary of, however, is that contagious 'buzz'. Everybody is susceptible – including the trade. But it is the buzz which will draw you over your set limit, so be careful not to be seduced by it.

3   The Sale

What You Need to Know from the Entry Form

THE LOT NUMBER ON THE SCREEN

Some auctions produce a catalogue of entry, but more often than not it is up to the purchaser to get out and find the cars on the yard. This is by far the best thing to do since it allows the eye to be drawn before the heart.

Many auctions give all the relevant information pertaining to the car on the windscreen and it is very important that the following at least is known:

a) Mileage on speedometer: is it correct?
    Has the car ever been a total loss?
    Date of registration or manufacture.

In addition, it is an advantage for a declaration to be made as to the following:

b) Chassis number
    Engine number
    Has this ever been a hackney carriage?
    Has this ever been a police car?
    Number of owners
    Direct fleet?

If the information is not on the screen – Ask! They may not tell you, but ask anyway. If you can't find out from the staff any of the above information (particularly that in category 'a'), then you should seriously consider whether your choice of auction house was a good one. Just don't make the mistake of expecting to be told a reserve! The best auction is a thorough auction. The lot should be displayed clearly in a well-lit hall or, preferably, in daylight.

Timing Your Entry

Cars should go up for auction in approximate numerical order. (Approximate is inevitable since cars that have not been driven for a while often have a flat battery which slows down the flow somewhat.)

In general, the auctioneer will sell at a rate of one lot per minute, and this is a fair guide to the length of time before your car will be offered. Remember to find out, however, at what number the lots begin. If the car you fancy is lot 252, it may be approximately 253 minutes before it is offered – unless, of course, the sale starts at lot 200! Asking avoids disappointment.

Offering

BUYING THE RIGHT LOT

The auctioneer will usually offer for sale the vehicle that stands immediately in front of the rostrum and should read out its lot number before he begins. As often as not he will make comments on the car as to its condition, mileage, etc., which should satisfy you that you are indeed bidding on the lot you wanted. Ninety per cent of the time it is obvious which car is being offered. Beware, however, of the following:

a) Catalogue sales – especially at commercial sales where items are offered before and after those that will be driven through. For instance, the auctioneer may have a van in front of him at the beginning of the sale, but may be offering plant items or HGVs, which are sold where they stand in the yard off-catalogue. When buying vehicles offered off-catalogue, you must inspect the vehicle carefully before the sale starts and be most attentive during the sale to ensure the lot number you wish to bid on is that which the auctioneer is offering. Should you mistake one lot for another, bid on it and buy it, you will be expected to pay for it. Sob stories do not wash with the auction staff.

b) Occasionally, a non-runner which is to be offered will be towed in to the auction hall by another vehicle. This is one of the few times when the vehicle that is not at the front of the queue is being offered. I remember one occasion when a well-known trader bid on a Cavalier with a cracked engine block. The auctioneer was surprised but it wasn't his job to question the bid and the vehicle was finally sold to him at what seemed to be very good money. The result was that a very unhappy trader was asked to pay up for what he had thought to be an amazingly cheap Range-Rover – the vehicle that had been used to drag in the Cavalier.

Auctioneers' Statements

When the auctioneer offers a vehicle he will make any pertinent announcement or statement regarding the vehicle. You must listen carefully to these statements, since you will not have a leg to stand on by claiming you were unaware of anything that was announced at the time of the sale. This verbal warning is binding and will be recorded on tape. Should you truly believe something serious has not been declared, then you may ask the auctioneer to re-play this tape to you – a long and tedious process, as you can imagine, which is best avoided.

Pertinent statements may include such things as:

VAT applicable (see Appendix 10)
New speedometer fitted, and when
Total loss
Source of vehicle
Ex-hackney
Ex-police
Radio or service history in office
Number of owners
Sold with/without trial

These are listed in what I consider to be descending order of importance.

The auctioneer should not comment on the condition of the vehicle (although often he will), nor say whether there is a service history in the car, since he probably doesn't know if there is one. Should such things be said, check for yourself. Never rely on the auctioneer's say-so, since this will only cause trouble later. You may only rely on what he tells you that you cannot check for yourself – as listed above. These points are mostly of a serious nature and the auctioneer will not make mention of them lightly. Anything else said in the way of casual banter is a tool to get a buzz going, and also to entertain the traders who have a long day ahead. It is important to distinguish between these important statements and a load of sales pitch!

Having made a statement about the vehicle that is being offered, the auctioneer will take what he considers to be sensible bids from the floor or else he will 'kick off' the bidding at a figure he considers to be sensible whilst still tempting enough to attract a useful flurry of bids from the crowd.

Sold, Not Sold or Provisional?

At some stage the bidding will peter out for one of three reasons:

a) SOLD – The lot is sold to the highest bidder under the hammer. The hammer will drop and the sale is complete.

b) PROVISIONAL – The highest bidder has reached a figure that the auctioneer deems to be close enough to the reserve or, more importantly, close enough to the vehicle's true value to be worth 'submitting' to the vendor. Usually he will announce the fact that the bid is 'provisional', and in any case he will still expect a deposit to be given. But he should never, if the bid is 'provisional', drop the hammer, which indicates a sale.

c) NOT SOLD – The bidding has not got to a level which the auctioneer deems worthwhile 'submitting'. This may be either because he feels the lot is worth more or simply because the reserve is far too high to be achievable.

'Trotting', 'Taking Out', 'Running'

Since auctions are not racing stables, this is a sensitive subject. However, although it is a thoroughly illegal practice, where it constitutes a 'mock auction', I believe it does go on in some places. Essentially, it involves the auctioneer running up the bidding by putting in false or non-existent bids, or occasionally taking bids from a vendor present at the sale who pretends to bid on his own car. By doing this the vendor and/or auctioneer hope to instil a false sense of security into the potential purchaser by making it appear that other people also have faith in the value of the car.

All this is bad practice and certainly is something you yourself should never indulge in. It is even debatable as to whether it has any effect, since some people can be put off rather than encouraged if they see another bidder. Furthermore, should you be found to 'buy in' your own car the auctioneer will undoubtedly frown upon it and may also charge you full commission on the sale – which he has every right to do.

None of this, however, should really worry the more discerning prospective buyer. The auctioneer will not risk pushing the bidding any higher than that which is a reasonable price for the vehicle, unless he feels sure that he has truly hooked his bidder. More to the point, he will (in practise) not risk losing his bidder once he has reached reserve price. His true goal is to sell the car and earn his commission.

The advantage to sensible 'trotting' i.e. an auctioneer bidding on a vendor's behalf, below reserve, (although I cannot condone it) is that there will be less time wasted, hopes dashed and vendors annoyed by continual submitting of bids at which they will not sell the car. To this end the auctioneer will only offer what is in his mind a reasonable bid. Bearing in mind that the prospective bidder should have set a limit, there is no reason to be particularly put off but every reason to attempt not to be 'hooked' and drawn any higher than necessary. Do your best to look totally disinterested and thus force the auctioneer to hold your bid as soon as he thinks it worthwhile, not to push on toward the reserve confident that you'll keep nodding away! Meanhile, keep a mind to the limit you have set.

Remember, a car sold under the hammer carries less

overhead for the auction in terms of time and telephone calls. Better still, it creates more opportunity for the auctioneer to produce that elusive 'buzz'.

To avoid being led on, it is important that you can distinguish between being 'trotted' and there being other genuine bids. The best thing to do is to watch the auctioneer like a hawk and, if possible, ask a friend to accompany you in order to spot the other bidder. The questions you must ask yourself are: is the auctioneer looking across to the same point each time, does he accept the bid before he looks (i.e. in anticipation), and can you spot the bidder?

At the end of the day, the ability to avoid 'trotting' is the difference between being a professional bidder and a one-timer wanting a vehicle for personal use. The professional might be able to save himself a few pounds by spotting this practice, but usually he will not be able to buy the car for much less than the novice because the reserve is ultimately the same for both bidders.

Bidding

There isn't much to be said about the act of bidding, but some thought should go into the manner of bidding. You will no doubt see if you keep your eyes peeled – and especially if you stand under the rostrum to where bids are being directed – some funny styles of bidding. Twitches of the eye, nods, a wave of a mobile phone, even by just staring traders will make their bid known to the auctioneer. Believe it or not, with a bit of practice it is very obvious to tell who is and who isn't actually bidding. So why the concealment? As I said before, nobody likes to bid on a vehicle alone. It makes them think they're offering too much. If you want the car it's best to keep quiet about it so that everybody else will think they're alone and will drop out. Either that or stand up, make yourself seen and bid like a true 'private' – with love in your eyes and a waving motion similar to that employed at an olympic stadium. This should be enough to make anybody give up in the knowledge that you'll pay anything to get your car. To be honest, I would say that the best approach is the former.

How to Bid Successfully

If you make a big show, then you will probably end up paying through the nose. The auctioneer will think you're hooked and 'trot' up to the reserve if necessary. Still worse, the trade may resent your presence and bid against you to 'make you pay for it'! I've seen it happen. Some bigger traders, especially in the commercial world, will even buy a vehicle that they don't want for more than it's worth, just to stop somebody else buying it – especially if that other person really needs a particular lot to run his business effectively.

You can imagine what a dream it is for an auctioneer to have two such people bidding against each other. Everything goes sky high over reserve, the commission rolls in and vendors roll over!

So, look disinterested but be prompt. Appear to have what you *have* got: a reserve of your own. Appear firm, decisive, and cold during the proceedings. Look as if you have to be there, as if this is work for you and not a shopping trip. In the extreme, it may even be worth dressing for the occasion – shirt and tie, jumper, trousers and an overcoat (preferably with Vauxhall or JPS on it!).

All in all, it is your duty to make the auctioneer certain of your ability to value a car. Make him believe you know exactly what you're doing and watch his eyes carefully as he will probably let on when he expects you to stop bidding by his expression. He will lose confidence – maybe the 'other' bid will come slower. Try fidgeting, act disinterested, pause a bit, bid again then turn and walk away.

Whatever you do *never* let anybody see you at an auction with a Parker's Guide. By all means have one and use one but never be *seen* with one. All private bidders have a Parker's Guide. All traders have a Glass's or CAP. If you can get hold of one of these 'trade only' publications from a friend, then you've cracked it!

One final point. Be decisive, not disappointed. I was on a rostrum not long ago and saw a car go down to a trader because the underbidder looked very uncertain and hung around too long. Finally, he couldn't get his hand out of his pocket, where his watch had snagged his coat, quickly enough. It may seem odd to you that the auctioneer wouldn't wait. True enough, but the car was over reserve, the trader had an account and would pay by cheque there and then. The private man was too much hassle to wait for. He was too slow. Although I was disgusted at the 'quick knock', it happens. So be confident, even if you aren't; pause for effect, but don't dither.

4   Trials

If your lot is sold under the hammer, then the contract of sale is binding. You may have the option of an hour test-drive and trial (if this was specifically offered) at the end of the sale, a process which is explained here.

When to Take Your Trial

This usually expires, in any case, an hour after the end of the sale – check the rules again. Furthermore, 'at the end of sale' is what it means, not because the staff are trying to be obstructive but because the vehicle has not been paid for and cannot be opened unaccompanied. You will have to wait until the sale is over and a member of staff from the yard is available. This may not sound like much time, but if you are at a large sale it might be four or five hours before you can have your trial, and then if you miss it you miss it.

Often it is possible to take your trial within the grounds, there and then, if you pay for the vehicle in full beforehand. This will entitle you to have the keys and give you the opportunity to check the car over for yourself. If you opt for this time-saver remember two things:

1) Never take the car off-site unaccompanied if you intend to bring it back with a complaint, especially if that complaint is that something is missing, like the spare wheel or radio – for obvious reasons.

2) If you do have a complaint covered by the terms of the 'end of sale trial', you will again have to wait until the end of the sale when the yard foreman or engineer can verify your problem is justified, and the manager or his assistant will be

able to deal with the problem. In this instance be patient. The auction staff are there to help not hinder, but they will remain impartial and must verify any claims you make – after the sale! The disadvantage now is that they have your money and you have a complaint. It is better to be patient and have your trial (on deposit) later!

Nearly every trial will only cover 'major mechanical defect' and you must understand that this is what it means. The components covered are usually listed either on the entry form or under the terms and conditions.

What Does the Trial Cover & How to Claim on it

Basically, the trial can be used to reject a car on the grounds of significant undeclared wear to:

Clutch – Steering – Engine – Transmission – Gearbox.

However, only when the engineer has verified the fault do you have a case. The trial covers *nothing* else.

When the engineer has agreed to your claim for rejection, you may now follow one of two courses:
1) claim back all the money (including indemnity); or
2) claim suitable 'chip' or reduction in price to cover repair of the ailing part.
Be sensible. If you are, this can result in a very fair settlement – especially if you know a handy mechanic!

To be compensated £200–£500, according to the problem, is not uncommon as long as you are sensible. Otherwise, the auctioneer or his assistant has the right to return your money without offering the 'chip' option to the vendor. Remember, the auction house is not responsible for this mess – the vendor is, and he will have to pay commission to the auctioneer whatever happens as long as the auctioneer can demonstrate that the purchaser has good grounds to complain. It is difficult business for the auction staff to handle. Be firm but always be pleasant and you will get the best out of the situation.

Should the auctioneer not allow your claim it may well be that you are in breach of the conditions or being too fussy. However, if you are still not satisfied then leave the car on site and return the next day with a qualified mechanic, preferably AA or RAC approved, to re-inspect the car and back you up if necessary. Always tell the auction staff what you intend to do and return any paperwork/keys you may have, retaining your receipt only. If you tell them and they know they are on thin ice you may save everyone a lot of effort – particularly yourself.

Should the situation occur whereby you leave the site, happy that your car has passed the trial, and something serious goes wrong, then try to ring the auction house straight away. This particular point highlights the advantages of paying on the day of sale, since as often as not the auctioneer will allow you back with a major mechanical problem as long as you are not too late i.e. not more than two hours after the sale. Remember, of course, as with any other talk of returns, you only have this option if you are entitled to a trial with the lot you buy.

Further Action

If the worst happens and you feel you have not been fairly treated, and the engineer you bring cannot sway the auctioneers, then you will need to do one of two things:
1) Wish you had gone to a more reputable auction, cut your losses, take the car, repair it or sell it again 'as seen'.
2) Go to Citizens' Advice, who will put you in touch with Trading Standards, and fight your case according to their advice.

Trading Standards are a powerful lot in the auction world. If the word is mentioned when all else fails and the auctioneer doesn't flinch you will probably find that he knows he is on solid ground. Re-assess whether you are expecting too much of the car – the trial is for 'excessive wear'. Modern cars have to be unlucky to suffer from excessive wear if they have been serviced properly. If this happens to be a fleet entry, it probably has been fully serviced.

Think before you throw the book and listen carefully to Citizens' Advice, remembering to take the Terms of Condition of Sale with you.

The Worthiness of a Trial

You're probably thinking by now that trials are pretty useless – but they rely on two things:
1) the extent of the problem and therefore the clarity of the claim;
2) the integrity of the 'insurer'.

Go to a good auction house and a trial may well be in your favour. Go to a very good auction house and bid on a Direct Fleet, full service history, one owner, warranted mileage car and I doubt if a trial will be necessary, nor will it be offered!

The main purpose of the trial rules is to prevent a rogue selling a car that does not work as being 'All good', 'Excellent throughout', etc., since if he tries it the buyer will reject the car with the auction's blessing. It is not designed to be testament to the car being as good as new, but it should help provide a serviceable unit.

5 Deposits and Payment Procedures

When your bid is successful the auctioneer will either drop the hammer on 'sold' bids or announce the sale as 'provisional'. Either way you will have to pay a cash deposit at the end of the rostrum. The amount of the deposit varies according to the auction. Generally it is £200, £500 or 10% of the sale price. Whatever the amount required, you must have it in order to bid. Don't expect the auctioneer to react well to tales of poverty, however temporary. If no deposit is forthcoming the car will be re-offered, usually straightaway, in order that any underbidder be given the chance to re-affirm his interest. It may be that the auctioneer knows the underbidder and is within his rights to call that bidder over to the rostrum and offer first refusal. Either way, he who has no deposit can forget trying to bid again. The auctioneer and manager will never again accept any bids from you. Believe it or not the memory for faces and names is long in the auction business, so make sure everything goes smoothly the first time!

Always ask before you bid what the procedure is once a bid has been taken.

Paying the Deposit

Once you have bid, your deposit is due and is usually payable at the rostrum. Having paid your deposit, you will have to give your name and address and you may be asked to sign the entry form to confirm that the figures written therein by the auctioneer represent in fact the sum you bid. Also check that the rest of the entry form tallies with the car you bid on – everybody makes mistakes, but nobody should sign for them!

Double check to see whether the trial is available and, if it is, take it as soon as you can (see Trials). If not, then the car is sold as you see it. Now go to the office via the canteen since the processing takes awhile.

Provisional Bids – What happens next

If your bid is provisional then the auction staff, and very often the assistant manager or representative whose customer it is the car belongs to, will ring that vendor and try their best to convince him or her of the merit of your bid. The same person will be trying to convince *you* that you should be offering more. Your big advantage is in having seen the car. If you like it still, having had another look since your bid, then offer him 'half way and no more' – after all, you can always go up.

Sometimes the poor chap on the other side genuinely will not be able to 'go back' with an increased bid but must get for his vendor what he has been asked for. I leave this to you, but remember it is easier for the man on the other side of the glass to do nothing than to work for you. Be nice, or you may get your deposit back rather suddenly!

On the other hand, if you do not want to bid any more, you are quite within your rights to take your deposit and go. If, however, you are not asked for any more money then that is it, the car is sold to you. It is as if you bought it 'under the hammer'. Do not be misguided into thinking that a provisional is two-way. Once your bid is accepted by the vendor, the car is yours. If the vendor wants more money you have the right then and only then to 'come off' the bid.

The provisional process can be quite drawn out and if your patience escapes you it will do no good. The auctioneer expects you to 'stand on' or wait until at least the end of the day. It is best to leave your phone number and, if for some reason you have changed your mind about the car, you can always hope that the vendor will want more money.

Payment – Where do you stand?

Given that the purchase goes ahead smoothly, you will then be requested to pay either by the close of business that day or by midday the next. If you do not comply then you will lose your deposit and the car will be re-offered. The reason for this is that the vendors must be told what they have sold and for how much, but a sold car is only sold when it is paid for. Furthermore, the auctioneers have to pay the vendor promptly, typically within three working days but occasionally even sooner.

This does not give much time for money paid into the auction account to clear before it is paid out again. Debtors can therefore cost a small fortune in interest, and indeed it is a hefty part of an auction's income that is made up of interest from other people's money on account for even a day or two!

Check, therefore, the time span in which you are asked to pay and make sure *before* your bid that you can meet it. There will also be a time limit on removal of your vehicle before penalties are attached. If you really have a problem go and ask the manager, who may be able to help, but pick your time. It is a stressful business serving at an auction counter when the sale has just finished, and everybody wants to pay and go. If it's a favour you need, bide your time. Ask when the pressure is off and I guarantee your chances of acceptance are 100% greater than if you go in at the peak!

One solution to prompt payment, but one that should be pre-arranged *with the auctioneers*, is to carry a cheque from a building society or bank for the amount and more that you intend to spend and to accept an auction cheque as change for the difference in value.

Finally, ask before you bid what payment consists of. They'll want money, of course, but nearly always in the form of: CASH, BUILDING SOCIETY CHEQUE OR BANKERS DRAFT. Beware of Bankers drafts. They usually cost about £10 per issue! Some auction houses are equipped for Switch, Visa, etc., these days, but *always ask*.

6 Arranging Finance for
Auction Purchases

Don't be put off buying at auction because you want to put your purchase 'on finance'. It is quite possible to arrange for payment to be made by means of a finance company cheque within the limits laid down by most auctions. Remember that, although this may seem more complicated and time consuming than the convenient arrangement of just signing an agreement at the forecourt and driving away, there are many advantages and savings to be made by arranging your own finance deals. For one thing, the overall cost of the deal that you arrange may well turn out to be considerably reduced because you have eliminated the middle man in the form of the trader who is usually on the receiving end of a handsome commission for signing you up. As we said before, the commission paid on such business is recoverable through the client, in the same way as that paid to an insurance salesman for arranging a personal pension.

Furthermore, you will by this method be in a position to choose your finance house for yourself, giving you (in my opinion) far greater peace of mind than would be the case if you simply accepted that which the dealer happens to be offering. You are, of course, also free to take advantage of the best deals available at the time. If finance is the route you wish to follow, then take the course of action below to ensure that the transaction passes as smoothly as possible. There is undoubtedly more work involved, as compared to the simple signing ceremony at the forecourt, but it is imperative that you remember what you want: to save money, and not to cut corners on the way. The key to a successful finance agreement is exactly that, AGREEMENT. You must communicate your requirements clearly with everybody involved at every stage in order to succeed.

1) Make all the necessary arrangements with your chosen finance company well in advance. Agree with them your planned method of purchase and highlight the time scales involved. You can tolerate no delays once your bid has been accepted and, given that you explain clearly the situation before it evolves, then usually there should be no problem in having the cheque raised the same day.

2) Ensure that the auctioneers are willing to assist you with the deal. Ask the general manager for his assistance well before the sale begins. Explain to him what you have arranged with the finance company and ensure that you raise your request for assistance early. Indeed, it is always best to talk of such matters the day *before* the sale (or on any non-sale day) in order that you can be assured of the manager's undivided attention.

3) Having been given the go-ahead by both the auction manager and, even more importantly, the financiers, you must now ensure that all the details of the agreement are available to give to the auctioneers. They will need a contact name at the finance company, telephone and fax number for that contact, and any relevant reference number. The contact at the other end must, obviously, be aware of all the arrangements, but less obviously it will be worth your while putting in a quick call to him or her before you bid to remind them of your case and ensure that they are actually in the office on the day.

4) Ensure you have an appropriate deposit for the sale that you attend. It may be a good time to pass on all the details of the deal when you give the deposit after bidding. Write them on a suitable piece of paper that can be attached to the entry form and remember to include any details your financiers may have dictated as to whom the invoice for the balance should be made out to. I find that finance companies are often very particular about what appears on an invoice, so make sure that any peculiarities are discussed with the

auctioneers when you ask their permission, and note them all down again at the fall of the hammer to hand in with your deposit. Your deposit will no doubt be forming part of the deal with the financier, as it is unlikely that you will have secured a 100% loan on a car.

One of two things might therefore apply in any case.

a) You need to present more than the auctioneer's deemed deposit value to satisfy the financier, in which case you will save the auction staff a lot of work if you hand this total sum in to form your whole deposit. Suffice it to say, however, that a deposit at an auction is just that, and it may be worth taking any trial you are due before committing such a large sum of money. If you are not due any trial, which is more likely the case, then it is a matter of keeping the auctioneer on your side by being as cooperative as possible now, in case there are any problems later.

b) You may have secured a loan demanding less than the auctioneer's deposit or none at all. In this situation the agreement is with the auctioneer and it must be reached *before* you bid. There is a good chance you will receive a satisfactory answer. If you do, ask that the auctioneer be advised or that you have some written confirmation to the effect that no deposit or a reduced deposit is acceptable. I suggest this for two reasons. First, because the auctioneer may be freelance and thus not party to your previous agreed course of action. Second, because any misunderstanding at the rostrum can bring out the worst in people, creating an irrevocable snap decision on the part of the auctioneer. These problems can always be avoided with a little forward planning.

All this may sound incredibly complex and daunting, but it really is not. All that I have done in this chapter is to highlight the shortfalls of not ensuring that the finance deal that you want to arrange has been clearly discussed with both parties, and that you have cleared the way to a comfortable solution of the whole. Of course the auction staff are indeed keen to sell cars, and the chances of your losing out by taking even the most uncooperative route are not any higher than if you take that attitude with any transaction. But all you have to do is *ask* to make the whole experience a day to remember and to be proud of when you add up what you saved.

The finance deal presents the auctioneer with the following problems:

1) Who to make the invoice out to.
2) Where to show the deposit given, i.e. whether to raise a receipt for the deposit and invoice the balance separately or show invoice less deposit in one.
3) Whether the finance company will pay indemnity fees as part of the deal. This may have to be shown separately.
4) What detail the finance company needs with regard to the vehicle it is buying, i.e. make, model, registration is usually shown on an invoice, but do they require mileage, number of former keepers, colour, engine c.c., etc.?
5) Who to send the finished invoice to, *by fax*, to arrange prompt payout.

Finance companies ask all these questions and more. Some even ask for condition reports. Remember, none of this is impossible to overcome. In fact a good auction has all the data on the entry form, but it is a huge help for the auctioneer to be told before he raises the first invoice exactly how it is to be done.

7 Choosing an Auction House

Take a Tip from the Vendors

In many ways the selection of an auction house can be more important for the vendor than the purchaser. It follows, then, that the reputation of an auction is borne out by the quality of vendor it attracts, and this by and large is true, assuming the auction house in question is reputable enough to be honest about who its vendors are!

Large companies like Boots, Nationwide Anglia Building Society, Nissan, etc., spend a lot of time and money creating a good reputation for themselves and are not likely to allow it to be tarnished by selling their used car fleet dishonestly, or by making false declarations as to its condition. Neither will they undertake to use any one auction house lightly. Indeed, research into the solvency of the auctioneer's company will be carried out by a large fleet vendor with some considerable care.

Should an auction house go bust just at the point that they were to pay out for vehicles sold on the vendor's behalf, then the vendor will find himself fighting along with all the other creditors for his money. Were the vendor to have been a large fleet disposal company, they may well be at risk of a considerable loss, having just sold perhaps ten or even two hundred vehicles at that critical moment! This research is pertinent to you as a purchaser should you need to claim on an auction house's indemnity reserve (see Chapter 8).

The only way to be sure of your auction is to read thoroughly a copy of their terms and conditions. This may appear to be a mammoth task, but it is a worthwhile practice. In addition, look at the declaration made on the windscreen. Make sure that the top copy, where displayed at all, has been properly completed in every case, whether by the vendor himself or by the auction house on behalf of the company. Should there be any gaps in the completion of the form then this should raise questions in your mind as to the effectiveness of the management on site, and perhaps to their honesty. For instance, the answer to the question 'Has the vehicle ever been a total loss?' is 'yes' or 'no', not 'never checked' or 'don't know'.

Any auction manager worth his salt will insist on every entry form being completely and unambiguously filled in if he is to avoid the kind of entry that nobody wants. Remember the entry form, and therefore its top copy, is a legal document admissible in court. Imagine only part completing your tax return by putting under income 'don't know', or missing your name out!

If the top copy is not correctly completed there isn't much chance for the part you *don't* see – like the vendor's name and address, for instance. Names and addresses are falsified for a number of reasons, none of them good. The vendor may, for instance, be trading cars and avoiding the tax man; worse, he may be stealing cars, selling 'total losses', undeclared clocking, etc.

One way to check this is to ask the auction staff, in the guise of a prospective vendor, whether it would be possible to collect cheques instead of having them sent by post. If the answer is yes, forget it! The only protection an auction house can offer is to post all cheques to make the life of the would-be crook as difficult as possible. Cheques should never be handed over the counter, nor should they be cashed by the auction staff, taken in part-payment for another car or paid into another account – hence the trend toward crossed cheques printed 'A/C payee only'.

Use your common sense whilst reading the paperwork in the windows of some of the cars. Anything declared as 'Direct' must *be* direct – not via one, two or three traders. You may laugh, but some of them try it time after time. This is where common sense comes in. If you find yourself at a scruffy little auction where you see an 'L' plate car and in the window 'Direct manufacturer, One Owner', is it really likely that the manufacturer would be using that auction direct?

Check number plates with declarations as to the source. Sometimes the name of the supplying dealer gives the game away. Often leasing companies advertise themselves in the rear window, which helps to confirm that the company from which the car is direct was a decent one.

Finally, the tyres on a fleet car all tend to be the same make, or at least not re-moulds. If in doubt, don't bother. There is always another auction around the corner, and it is important that the one you are using is honest.

Society of Motor Auctions

Most auction houses are honest. As with many service industries, there is an organization to which I would recommend any auction you consider using should belong as a pre-requisite.

The Society of Motor Auctions was set up by an ex-auction man with a view to bringing all auctions together once a year for meetings and discussions beneficial to everyone. One of the most useful things to emerge from this association is that to join it one has to be thoroughly vetted by people who understand the business. What is more, the Society offers a service by which any auction member may report loss by theft, non-payment on account, or any other warnings felt relevant. The Society then investigates and faxes the details to all the member auctions. In this way member auctions can keep an eye open for stolen cars and have some control over bad debtors.

8 Indemnity

What is it and How Does it Work?

Indemnity is a fee added to the purchase price of every vehicle registered for use on the road that is sold through car auctions. The fee varies and often works on a sliding scale according to the value of the transaction. It is usually about £40 + VAT for the first £1,000 of the sale price and up to £5 per each additional thousand. The purpose of the fee is as the name suggests. Having paid what is effectively a 'premium' to the auction house, they will indemnify the purchaser against:

1) any claim made against the purchaser for Hire Purchase outstanding on the vehicle at the point of sale;
2) the vehicle ever having been a total loss (i.e. sustained over 50% damage);
3) the vehicle having been stolen and sold again by a vendor not having due title;
4) the mileage (where declared warranted only) not being genuine.

This protection is usually provided not, as may be thought, through purchase by the auction house of indemnity insurance but through the auctioneer's own indemnity fund into which the indemnity fees are paid. This explains why VAT is often charged on the sum.

The sum should, if the auction site has been run properly, rarely be used and, with indemnity reserves seldom drawn on, the fund itself soon grows to a substantial sum on which the auction house earns good interest.

The indemnity system operated by auction houses is, in my opinion, an excellent protection for the purchaser of a used car and, to my knowledge, not easily beaten in terms of simplicity and satisfactory performance.

Making an Indemnity Claim Easier

The reason the system is so effective is that, in the majority of the cases, the money being returned to the purchaser is neither that of the auctioneer nor of his fund. The nature of the cover provided usually encourages a purchaser to complain promptly should there be a problem with the vehicle's integrity, at which point the auctioneer holds the funds received from the transaction until he has established the facts of the case.

Where the purchaser is entitled to his money back the auctioneer will pay it (less the indemnity fee in many cases) without a claim to his indemnity fund, since he has not yet paid out the sale price to the original vendor. Alternatively, a reduction in price may be negotiated. Whichever the case, the auction house itself does not lose money as long as the case is raised early enough after the sale, i.e. within 48 hours or so, in time to hold payment.

To this end many auctions have introduced clauses in their terms and conditions of sale demanding that the purchaser compare the chassis or Vehicle Identification number (VIN) on the vehicle with that recorded in the Vehicle Registration document and report any discrepancies therein within 24 hours. Similarly, if the vehicle is sold 'log book to follow', the purchaser is then required to check the same within 24 hours of receipt of the log book. If this condition is not complied with and a later claim arises which could have been raised earlier through this simple check then the indemnity is deemed invalid.

The moral of the story is to make sure that any possible checks are carried out as soon as possible after the sale. The easier the financial perspective of the auction house, the less hassle will come out of it.

Drawing from the Fund

So when does the indemnity fund actually get used? There are only so many things that can be checked straight away (as we will soon see), and occasionally problems raise their ugly heads sometime later. For example, HP outstanding can be difficult for the auction house to check thoroughly, even though they pay a fee to 'HPI' every car before they issue a cheque to the vendor.

HPI are a company specializing in holding on computer file three items of information against a registration number:

1) Hire Purchase outstanding and finance house involved.

2) 'VCAR' or Vehicle Condition Alert Register on which a registration will show if the associated vehicle has been reported subject to an insurance claim. This is the register that defines 'total loss' in many auctions.

3) Security Alert Register and Police Station contact – vehicles registered as having been stolen.

Accessing this information requires that a fee is paid and, although the amount varies with the number of enquiries and method of access, this adds up to quite a bill before long!

The service is also available to the man in the street under the trade name HPI Autodata for the sum of £15 + VAT per enquiry. I would recommend that anybody not buying a car from auction or buying from an auction at which indemnity is not chargeable should take up this service, as £15 is a small price to pay to ensure a relative measure of safety.

So why isn't it foolproof? The catch is that UK insurance companies are not obliged to register Hire Purchase agreements with anybody. Nor are they obliged to declare settlements on vehicles involved in major accidents. The onus is, quite rightly, on the vendor to do this, with obvious results. HPI, therefore, rely on insurance companies to register information with them of their own free will. This happens ninety-nine times out of a hundred because it is in the interest of the insurance company to do so. Similarly, stolen cars and those that have had total loss damage are not ones which insurance or finance companies want to be involved with.

HPI will advise the insurer if another insurer already has an interest in a particular car, thus preventing multiple HP agreements. HPI is constantly being informed of progress on HP accounts, and their income is generated from collation and sale of this data.

What HPI *cannot* do, however, is guarantee that any information they issue will be wholly correct and up-to-date. There are small loopholes through which a vehicle can show as clear on the HPI register when in fact it is financed up to the ears.

If this information should surface later, then the HPI company will send you a letter, advising you that the vehicle they declared clear has actually got a sum outstanding and did so on the date of sale. It's the auction that loses, for your indemnity covers you for this eventuality.

Another problem area which HPI are currently tackling, along with DVLA, is a change in number plate. All enquiries are made on registration mark and model, but if, say, an Escort with a private plate was put on finance, and then that plate was transferred to another Escort *without* finance, the finance stays with the original vehicle. This means that although the vehicle now bears a new plate, the finance on it is recorded on the old plate. This can get quite tricky!

HPI are developing a system of checking plate changes. However, to my knowledge, auctions do not use this service extensively, probably because they know the source of the bulk of their vehicles (which is the key to everything).

Indemnity and Choice of Auction House

The moral of the story is that, whatever you do to try and check the car thoroughly there and then, you may still fail. But if you have paid an auction indemnity and complied with the requirements of that indemnity, you are definitely better off – unless your auction house goes bust, at which point indemnity funds will be used (as with any other asset) to pay off creditors.

Your best bet is to choose an auction group with a good balance sheet, low debt and an indemnity scheme that is simply explained in the terms and conditions, i.e. choose a large, well managed group such as NCA, ADT or CMA.

Total Loss and Indemnity

DEFINING A TOTAL LOSS VEHICLE

Here we are on rocky ground. Basically, any vehicle so
registered with HPI on the VCAR will be classed by any
auction as a total loss. There are vehicles that manage to
avoid this classification. Owing to the likely nature of their
repairs (probably on the cheap and not through recognized
bodies), they are the worst of the bunch.

Many an auction manager will refuse an audience with
anybody claiming their vehicle to be a total loss undeclared,
unless they can prove it. If the vehicle is not on the VCAR,
the onus is on the purchaser to show that there is a cause for
concern.

PROVING A TOTAL LOSS

A trip to a VIBRA appointed agent is a start. Have an
inspection carried out as to the extent of the damage that
you feel defines the total loss. Remember that the repairs to
the car must amount to at least 50% of the value of the
vehicle at the time it is repaired – *not* 50% of the sum you
paid. No doubt the inspector will give you a good idea of
what the repairs might have cost at the time.

The next problem is to establish when the repairs
occurred. Try ringing the previous owners in the log book as
far back as possible. Often the person who repaired the car
is not in the book but 90% of the time the people you speak
to will be most helpful, if a little surprised.

If possible, get some written information sent to you, and
as you build up a case collect as much documentation as
possible to present to the auctioneer. You must be able to
show his vendor – or, should your claim be late, his bosses –
why they should pay back the money. The auctioneer won't
be convinced by a red-faced screaming banshee pointing at a
piece of slightly buckled metalwork under the bonnet of the
offending car – after all, total loss is total loss, and nearly
every car has had the odd bump.

It is rare to be lumbered with a total loss that cannot be

shown to have been one. Once you have proved it convincingly enough, the return of your money is only a matter of time, either amicably through the manager or – if your selection of auction has been unwise – through a trip to Trading Standards!

If you cannot show the car to be a total loss then probably, unless you are incredibly unlucky, it isn't.

FURTHER ACTION

If you feel hard done by, always approach Trading Standards. They have access to a lot more information than you and can undoubtedly help, or at least put your mind at rest.

If you have been told repeatedly and at length by an unswerving manager or assistant that there is nothing wrong with the car, a tip worth remembering is to turn around and tell him that, in that case, they won't mind selling the car through their auction. If he has anything to hide his heart will sink and his face turn pale as he envisages yet more hassle, next time, possibly, from a more important customer. It's not guaranteed to gain much ground – but I expect it would be satisfying enough to set you on your way to Trading Standards!

9 Choosing Your Car and Making a Move

Matching Needs Against Desire

Now that you know how an auction operates, the question remains: which of the many cars lined up on the yard should you be sinking your hard earned cash into?

No doubt an idea of the sort of car you want will be drifting about in your head, perhaps since childhood. But consider first whether the luggage space in the Porsche that has always been your heart's desire will suit your three children, two dogs and five mountain bikes!

This book is by no means designed to help you choose between the many makes and models available, so let us assume that a decision has been made as to the particular model desired by you, the prospective purchaser.

Now forget it.

By all means go to the auction with a specific model in mind, but don't expect either to find exactly what you're looking for straight away, or to be lucky enough to find the perfect specimen. Life is made much easier if you keep a fairly open mind at first.

Consider what the vehicle is to be used for most of the time and how you need it to perform, what you can afford to spend on the purchase and, more importantly, what will be the running costs. Having done this, you will come up with at least two or three manufacturers who produce a model to suit your specific needs. The two or three you decide upon will be very similar, and from here your personal preference will no doubt be reflected in the price you're willing to pay. Next, check the cost of insurance for your choice, and the next higher specification equivalent, where appropriate. One young couple had to return an Orion Ghia and re-sell it after discovering, too late, that they could not get insurance for it at all. (To avoid this problem ring Freephone RAC – see Appendix 2.) Always get an insurance quote before you buy.

Finding Your Model

Now let your fingers do the walking, especially if you are buying your first or only car. Auction houses are often sited at fairly remote locations, usually owing to the acreage they require for storage. The larger the auction you choose the more likelihood there is of your particular model being represented. It is obviously to your advantage if there are two or three of the same model available at once, since this affords a choice and guides your valuation as you watch similar lots being sold.

Telephone the auction and find out the following:
1) When are the fleet cars offered?
2) How many are being offered? (They may be cagey on this!)

Invariably fleet sales are held during the day. This may be a problem for the private buyer, but it's one very much worthwhile overcoming.

Take a day's holiday to buy a car and get a good one. The evening and Saturday sales which you will no doubt be told about are run by the auction with the specific intention of attracting private buyers. The entry usually consists of the cars that were not sold during the fleet sale, because their reserve was too high for the trade, and trade cars which have no doubt been bought from a fleet sale, polished up, and re-offered to you at a profit.

If a car is too expensive for the trade, why should you pay for it instead? The buying power of any private customer against that of a trader or wholesaler is far greater, whatever the market-place. Use this to your advantage. Attend a day sale and outbid the trade on the prime fleet cars rather than give them profit on the same car two days later!

Continuing your line of questioning, probably now on the afternoon of the day prior to the sale, ask the auction house at what point the fleet cars that are to be entered will have arrived on site and their details become available. Ask for instance, 'Do you have any Vauxhall Cavalier, 1.6L, 5 Door, either '89 or '90 G plate?' If you can be as specific as possible, then the person on site will be able to help you much more efficiently.

What they will need is an idea of the make, model, age and acceptable mileage of the car you require, whether it should be an automatic or manual and the number of doors. Colour comes later! Don't expect the auction staff to be particularly conversant with every shade in the colour spectrum – for instance, Wedgewood Blue is a far cry from Tasman Blue. No doubt they'll tell you just 'blue' – often from the detail on the log book.

If any contenders come up, then work from a list to extract the information you need since there is nothing more frustrating than realizing that you have forgotten to ask some pertinent point as the phone goes down.

Ask for:

Model and number of doors
Registration letter
Date of registration
Colour
Mileage
Is the mileage warranted?
Service history – full or part, if any.
MOT (where applicable, and due three years after registration)
Tax
Has the vehicle ever been a total loss?
Number of owners
Is it direct from Fleet?

Making a Move – What you will need

Having done this, it won't be too tricky to decide whether it is worth the trip. There is no doubt that it is worthwhile attending a few auctions before you bid, but no trip is worth making unless it can potentially bear results.

Check, now, what form of deposit is required, when payment deadline is reached and what indemnity fee would be payable should you buy the car. Asking for the indemnity fee can, in all innocence on the part of the auction staff, be a useful guide as to the reserve price – a closely guarded secret!

By asking the above list of questions you will have drawn the eye of the person you are talking to down to the entry form, and it would be a surprise if that person missed noticing the reserve. Asking the rate of indemnity can therefore be a help. The inexperienced member of staff will probably tell you that the figure you will be requested to pay will be, say, either £29 or £30 plus VAT. Jot this down and when you get to the auction hall look for a list of indemnities – these often run in scales of £1,000 or £500 of purchase price. The answer you've been given will put you near one or other price boundary. For example:

Sale Price	Indemnity
Up to £249	£27 + VAT
£250 – £499	£28 + VAT
£500 – £999	£30 + VAT
£1,000 – £1,499	£32 + VAT
etc. …	

Thus, if you've been told £30 or £32 plus VAT, the vehicle must be reserved around the £1,000 mark.

Unfortunately, the more wary and experienced staff member is wise to this and will quote a 'sliding scale from £27 to £34, according to the sale price, but no more than £34 in your case'. However, it is well worth asking.

Armed with your deposit, a trip to the auction seems imminent.

FIRST IMPRESSIONS COUNT

Walk out among the cars aligned for sale. Your eye will be drawn to three or four bright and shiny cars which stand out from the rest. Close inspection will probably reveal that, of

the four, three of these will have been 'valeted' or 'bulled' up
to the nines and are probably trade entries.

The other one will no doubt be thick with new paint –
probably still wet! Keep looking and among what is left you
will begin to spot the difference between these shiny,
squeaky-clean cars and the really genuine fleet entry, which,
whilst looking driven in and 'straight off the road', appears to
have been looked after properly. Try to train your eye to spot
the car that, although not valeted to showroom standard, has
a gleam that indicates somebody has been attending to it.

After a little experience you'll be able to pick these cars out
from the rest, just as you noticed those three or four extra
shiny cars on that first day. Practise this technique in the local
car park, on the street, everywhere you go. Look at your own
or perhaps your neighbour's car, one that you know to have
had tender loving care, and compare it to others. It is
surprising how quickly one can learn to 'spot' a genuine car,
with its original paint, some realistic small chips from stones
off the road, and the potential to really shine with a good
valet.

Establishing Source

Now establish the source of a car that has caught your eye.
Hopefully you will agree by now that the car you should be
bidding on is one directly entered for sale by one previous
owner – either a direct fleet entry or a well cared for
privately owned and entered vehicle. From the point of view
of 'money is no object' servicing, the direct fleet entry is
preferable.

What is more, you should be at an auction house that
either displays information in the windscreen or is happy to
give it on request. Look for the words: 'direct from the fleet'
or 'one company owner direct'.

Do not accept as direct company any statement implying
that there is a 'company' behind the entry, e.g. 'sold as seen,
company policy' with no statement indicating the word
'direct'. Traders run companies, and they are quite within
their rights to sell cars that they are trading under the
banner: 'company policy, sold as seen'.

You can be sure that any car entered direct from the company will clearly advertise the fact since the auctioneers know that this is a very positive selling point. Do not be drawn into making assumptions or reading anything into any statement made at an auction. The facts are there, clearly presented, to help sell the car.

The Log Book's Story

Next check to establish whether the car is being sold with its V5, or 'Vehicle Registration document' – its 'log book'. Often, as previously described, log books for fleet vehicles are said to be 'to follow', but make sure that they are going to appear. Should you purchase a car 'log book to follow' you should chase the auction for it, and they will in turn chase the company concerned.

The log book tells a story in itself.

Should you have opted to buy a non-fleet entry or perhaps an older car, then it is useful, if possible, to have a look at the log book. I would strongly advise against buying any car that has not come from a large fleet or finance company if it is sold without a log book or declared as 'V5 to be applied for'. Even though the auction will be indemnifying you against any problems with regard to legal title, there is no way of reading the log book's story if it isn't available to be read!

Look for a log book that is clean and tidy, without dog-ears and, notably, one that has not been stapled full of holes in one or other corner – all these are indications that the car has changed hands a good few times. The latter is an indication that the log book has been attached to an auction entry form before, but what it really means is that the number of former keepers described on the log book is probably not that accurate. If the same old tatty log book has been passed from pillar to post it must be obvious that it hasn't been to Swansea for some time and, therefore, that the previous owners have not registered their ownership. Worse, it may be that this is the original log book showing, say, two owners from new, whilst another more up-to-date log book has been issued to a third owner. Suddenly, when you put your name in the log book, your new V5 will read four owners from new instead of three. There will be no come back with the auction unless a declaration as to the number of owners was made at the point of sale.

Avoid grubby old log books. Try to buy a car whose documentation has stayed in one file for its entire life – a true one owner. The V5 is a much more important piece of paper than just a medium through which police can issue you with a speeding fine! It has a direct bearing on the history and, therefore, the value of your car.

Having established the number of owners and the source of the car, compare the mileage on the odometer with that on the entry form. Find out whether this declared mileage is deemed correct, and be wary of declaration of a new speedometer having been fitted. This should be made clear and will, hopefully, be all over the top copy of the entry form as displayed in the car.

10   A Valuation

Mileage

If the mileage is 'not correct', then four things may be the case:

1) The company selling the car is not willing to involve itself with disputes that may arise over mileage when incorrect declaration has been made, i.e. it really is 'company policy' not to get involved in warranting mileages, because of the seriousness of the possible repercussions on any mistakes made. If this is the case, the company will almost undoubtedly be a large one and probably in the public eye, able to afford incredible losses from their vehicles in favour of protecting their 'good reputation'. There are, surprise, surprise, considerably less of these vehicles being sold these days, but where they occur the auctioneer is liable to comment on their decision to offer the vehicle in this way!

2) The vehicle has had a new speedometer, but it is not certain exactly when this occurred. Usually records exist to show at what mileage speedometers were fitted and the present reading is added to the original to give a warranted mileage – all of which is declared on the entry form.

3) The vehicle has been 'round the clock', in which case 100,000 should be added to the mileage. It is more and more common nowadays, however, for manufacturers to fit six figure odometers.

4) The car has been 'clocked', i.e. the mileage has been turned back on a tidy high mileage vehicle to give the impression that it is in fact 'low mileage'. No doubt the service history will have disappeared into the bargain.

Checking steering wheels and pedal rubbers, play in steering, carpet wear, seat sagginess etc. is the answer to spotting a clocked car. But with profit margins increasing more and more, those involved in this criminal activity are not adverse to replacing all worn-looking parts in order to fool the wariest bidder. This car will probably be sold 'log book to be applied for' so that by the time you have rung the previous recorded owner and established the truth the vendor will have disappeared with his money, leaving you to fight it out with the auction over an indemnity claim. Rocky ground indeed, because the auctioneer will try to show that the vehicle was not misrepresented as such and you are likely to find yourself involved in a long wrangle.

Avoid, where possible, mileages that are *not* warranted. There are so many reputable companies with excellent computerized records detailing services and mileages throughout a car's life, all selling their fleets with warranted mileage whenever they can, that there is no need to risk getting involved with the few who cannot give their support to their vehicle's worth. Remember, 50,000 miles added to 30,000 showing on a Sierra 1.6L 90G represents some £2,000 off its value. Mileage has a real effect on price.

The Service History

The service history is the guide to a car's history that we have all been looking for – similar to the difference between the odd bone found at an archaeological dig and the sort of information that comes out of the Domesday book. The full service history speaks volumes. The service should be regular and the mileages logically increasing with time.

From a valuation point of view the servicing of a car varies in importance according to the make and model of the vehicle in question. Having a full service history for a Yugo may increase its value marginally, but having a full service history for a high mileage Mercedes 500 SEL will make a difference of perhaps £6,000, depending on who you ask!

If you are looking at purchasing anything 'lumpy' – either top of the range Vauxhall, Ford, etc., or, more importantly, Audi, BMW and prestige cars like Mercedes, Jaguar and

Rolls Royce – then the full service history is of increasing importance. In fact without one, the car may not be worth considering at all. If full service is not forthcoming then it is imperative that the true and unquestionable history of the car is known, with special regard for mileage. This goes for all cars but none so much as the prestige ones. When valuing anything like an Audi, BMW or Rolls Royce, expect to be asked at every juncture, 'What service history has it got?'

MOT

Often a company car is sold without MOT, even though one may turn up in the post with the 'following' log book. Either way a car in need of an MOT is no use to the private buyer because, without it, it cannot be taxed.

The solution to this, then, is to get the car MOT'd. It is currently illegal to drive a car on the road without MOT unless you are only driving it to a pre-arranged MOT test or to a garage for pre-arranged repairs to make it roadworthy. If you are in doubt, check first with your insurance company, or the police.

The MOT test has been tightened up recently, with very strict controls introduced in April 1993. Any vehicle sold without an MOT will have an effect on your valuation of it, in order that sufficient funds are withheld to carry out any repairs necessary for it to meet MOT regulations.

One new requirement that is quickly checked and extremely pricey is that the windscreen must not be cracked, clipped or scratched within the sweep of the wiper blades. A new windscreen for any car is a good £150, and for executive and sports models it may cost three times this figure.

Valuations

Having discovered the year and registration prefix of the car, established that it has been declared as never having been a total loss, and checked that it stands in plenty of good daylight, a valuation must be reached. You will need to know whether the mileage is deemed correct, the extent of any service history and existence of MOT for cover over three years old (see above).

INSPECTION FOR VALUATION

It is important to inspect your prospective purchase in good daylight. It should be washed clean in order that the paintwork can be properly scrutinized, and it *must* be dry. Rain drops on a polished car can make any old scrap-heap look beautifully shiny and scratch free. In fact it has been known for vendors of cars to squirt the body work with a spray bottle full of water just as they go into the auction hall!

The first thing to do is to check whether the car has ever been re-sprayed. If paintwork has been carried out, then to what extent, and more importantly – why. Presumably it's been done because of some form of damage. The condition of paintwork and panels of a car are like its log book – they tell a story which adds to your gradually growing picture of its history.

By looking along the length of the car you should see the light catching the panels of doors and wings in a smooth, clear manner reflecting in the background images of the nearest objects so that no distortion occurs. There will undoubtedly be small dents and scratches caused by stones or car-park door-opening sessions, but look for crazed or thick paint lacking that glazed look of a new billiard ball.

Were you to enlarge the surface of a re-sprayed panel then the difference between that and a factory finish would perhaps be similar to the difference between a red snooker ball and a red golf ball. That is the look you are chasing, reflected in the light. It isn't easy to spot until you've seen it once before!

Stand back from the car and look for variation in the colour of the paint that gives the game away. Coach lines may be missing where a panel has been re-sprayed. Even the most obvious things like trim not having been replaced may be staring you in the face. Remember that if one panel is re-painted then the next will probably be purposefully oversprayed to merge them. Also, to cover one door skin the professional will paint the whole side of a car.

Check the door rubbers and handles: lift the handle and check that the plastic underneath is still black. Put your fingernail under the rubbers of the windscreen and rear screen. Lift them and check that there is no ridge of thicker paint where the rubber stops.

Overspray onto trim, inside of wheel arches, tyres, shock absorbers, bumpers, is the most likely give-away. Look for anything not the same colour as the paint and see if it has any spray on it.

Whilst scrutinizing your panels you may find faint circular lines in the paintwork, hardly noticeable at a distance, that look like contours on a map. Run your fingers gently over the bodywork to make your discoveries. Circular lines in the paintwork, along with very minor pock marking of the surface (that golf ball effect), are sure signs of filler!

Check for ripples in the metal work which show signs of strong forces at play, especially in the roof area around the corners and at corners of factory-fitted sun-roofs. Once the car is being driven through the sale similar defects must be searched out under the bonnet and especially under the carpet of the boot.

Ripples in the car's shell may well indicate major accident damage and possibly a twisted chassis. Where any suspicion of mis-shapen roof or door pillars arises, then forget the deal and start again elsewhere.

Having checked the car over, the decision as to its condition remains with the purchaser. Where paintwork has been found you may have filler. If the paintwork is extensive around the front or rear end, then probably accident damage is the cause. In this case the quality of the repair must come into consideration. Where the accident damage appears to be extensive enough to have required paint over both wings and bonnet, front doors and pillars, then surely the structural integrity of the car must be questioned. Another car will turn up.

Your inspection should convince you that the car is structurally sound from an accident point of view. Given that the inspection passes muster, then a valuation must be reached. There may be panels, in particular the bonnet, where stone-chipping is prevalent and for this to be put right you may consider having the car professionally painted in places.

An estimate of approximately £100 per panel to be properly painted should be about right. Be a little more pessimistic where metallic paint is concerned. Remember – a bad paint job is worse than no paint job.

MOTs can be costly to pass these days, and any car not having a current MOT should sell for at least £400 less than a similar one which does.

Use these estimations to subtract from the value you finally reach.

Arriving at a Figure

Valuing cars is an ongoing, ever-changing judgement determined by the particular items you are faced with and the market-place in which you are operating. In order to get a reasonable figure, however, the following procedure might be followed:

1) Inspect the vehicle in question and calculate an adjustment to be made for its condition and existence and length of MOT as described previously. Establish the exact model, any extras (sun-roof, electric windows, etc.), the mileage (and whether it is correct), the exact age and whether or not the car has ever been a total loss. Also consider the extent of its service history (see section on service history).

2) Study the classified advertisements in trade magazines, local papers and any other listings you may be able to get hold of. Draw up a decent number of sample prices of the same model with similar mileage and of the same age. Average out these prices and arrive at a retail price figure for the car. Then deduct approximately 20% of this price.

3) Using Parkers Guide or a similar used car price guide, check the price listed for your particular vehicle and mileage. Subtract from this guide price those sums that were drawn up under part 1. Compare this figure with that arrived at in part 2.

4) Telephone two or three auctions and ask for a valuation. Remember, auction houses only make money when they sell cars on behalf of vendors. There is no reason why you should not pretend that you are a vendor with a specific car

to sell and interested in a free valuation.

Describe the car using details of model, year, mileage, number of owners etc., plus general condition, and the auctioneer or his assistant will undoubtedly give you a reasonably accurate estimate of what the car would be expected to fetch at auction. Expect to be asked how many owners the car has had, the exact model, auto/manual, colour, sun-roof, condition. Although the auctioneer may be inclined to exaggerate the price slightly with a view to enticing you and your entry on site, this is generally a useful guide.

5) Telephone an auction and see if you can establish roughly what one might expect to pay for the car you have in mind. Again, you will get a slightly biased estimate, but this time the bias may well be toward undervaluing! Much of this work can be done in advance, and after attending a few auctions you will become quite capable of valuing your choice of car to within £200 or so.

Remember, all the fuss about valuation stems from the fact that a trader may have only £500 profit in a car, if that, if he trades solely through auctions. Thus he has to be able to value the car to within £100. You, on the other hand, could be saving in excess of £1,000 by not buying retail, so the importance of valuing the car with pinpoint accuracy is not so great.

Now a word of caution. Having realized just how much you stand to save, the most dangerous and most common mistake when buying at auction is to get carried away with the savings made. Just because you are spending so much less does not mean that the difference should be put towards a faster, larger, nicer car. You will undoubtedly need to carry out one or two minor repairs or replacements to the car during its first service, and if you are unlucky you may have to fall back on the money saved to make right an unseen problem.

Fingers crossed, the money saved *will* be saved, but it is very important you keep it until that saving is a fact.

11   Final Inspection of Bodywork and Mechanics Prior to Sale

Unless you are lucky, especially charming, or both, you are unlikely to get the keys to a car before it goes through the auction. Since nearly all cars offered, and especially those sold from the fleet, are sold as seen, it is important that you make sure you have 'seen' them to the best of your ability.

There are reams of books written about how best to evaluate the mechanical condition and roadworthiness of used cars, but this is not one of them. There are, however, a few tricks worth knowing which are used by long-standing trade purchasers at auction, simply because the environment is a little different – i.e. no time!

First, there is no excuse for not having checked, in good light, the body and paintwork as described previously. By applying a certain amount of common sense, a good eye and sensitive touch, you should be able to spot any paintwork or patching up that has been carried out. It is always worthwhile, from a body and paint point of view, to leave the car and come back after a cup of tea for a second look. It is surprising how often the most obvious thing was missed out in the first examination. I once scrutinized the paintwork on an Orion for a client. It was only on passing the same car again that I noticed a whole strip of trim missing!

Some Simple Checks on Bodywork etc.

1) All doors should be hung correctly, with coach lines and mouldings aligning nicely.

2) Bonnet and boot should fit snugly into the gap between the wings. Should there be any sign of the gap being wider on one side or the other then check the other gaps around the wings to make sure they are evenly spaced (i.e. between wing and door pillar, headlamp, front grill, etc.). It may be that a new wing has been fitted. It may also be that the bonnet or boot lid have simply been knocked out of alignment. Only by checking all round the panel in question and remembering to hunt out overspray will you know which is the case.

3) Look for unconformities in the undercoat underneath the car, especially around jacking points, floor pans and boot floors with a view to checking for any new areas which will appear blacker and fresher. Also look very carefully for lines of welding anywhere underneath the car that appear to run for long distances across the vehicle.

4) Check the tyre treads. (The insertion of a 20p piece should not reveal the shoulders of the next bevels.) The bigger the car the more expensive the tyre, and any which need replacing should be taken into consideration. If you notice that any of the tyres are re-moulds – signified by the symbol (R) and Re-mould written on the sidewall – then you should, in my opinion, budget to replace them with a good make of new tyre.

5) Whilst checking the tyres also check the rims of the metal wheel itself. Often people inadvertently clip the kerb with the rim of their wheel and it buckles. This can cause all sorts of trouble and the rim should be replaced. No doubt the scrap-yard can supply a cheap rim whilst you run on the spare in the meantime, but remember this happens to alloy wheels too, which is a different story. Alloys are harder to replace and therefore expensive.

6) Tap the sills. If you think there is any chance of decay, use a heavy metal object to establish whether there is a problem. The solid metallic clang will drop a few tones to a dull thud where problem areas occur.

Suspension

An easy test to check that the shock absorbers are O.K. is to bounce the car by leaning on and off the body just above the shock to be tested. Once the car is bouncing nicely, stop pushing and watch. If the shock absorber is functioning the car should settle within 1½ oscillations.

Checking Mechanical Failure

The only opportunity you will have to complete your bodywork, electrical and mechanical checks will be whilst the car is being driven through. Once the driver appears with the keys you should observe the following procedures:

1) Watch and listen as the car is started. Any emission of blue smoke should promptly clear. Listen to the engine for sounds of knocking – a deep clonking or clattering noise means wearing on either the bottom or top of the engine respectively.

2) Ask for the bonnet to be lifted. Check again for clattering noise over and above that of the engine firing. This may indicate either a big end running or a cam shaft worn. This is your most important check. Wear here ranges from £300 to a new engine. If the wear is severe, you will hear a clear clattering like stones in a plastic drum being rolled over. (See Section 2 of Chapter 14.)

3) Under the bonnet check the wings. If they have been replaced there will be overspray into the engine components and the sealant along their edge will look roughly smoothed as if with a knife rather than properly finished in a worm-like form. Check for any buckling of the inner bodywork where panels inside the engine compartment have been literally knocked into shape, revealing areas of flaking paint and bare metal. This may indicate a previous front-end collision.

4) Still under the bonnet, lift off the oil filler cap. The underside of the cap should be oily and black. If it is a thick creamy white then this indicates water in the oil, which may be through a breached head gasket or a cracked head at worst. Head gaskets can easily be replaced (£50–£100) but if the head is warped or cracked you may be in for expensive grinding or a new part (£150 + +).

Cover the filler hole with your palm and hold for 30 seconds. No significant pressure should build up, and when your hand is removed there should be only a modest puff as slight pressure is released. Should a huge burst of air blow out then there is a good chance you will also see a bit of blue smoke from the exhaust, indicating worn piston rings. At best this will mean new rings in the future, at worst a re-bore. The difference could be between £100 and £500!

5) By now the engine should be warmed up a bit and running smoothly. Should there be any mis-fire then try removing one plug lead at a time until no effect is had on the engine's tone. If this happens the plug which had no effect is faulty and the problem is a simple one. If you find a change in tone whichever plug lead is removed, then this might imply a compression problem – a test for which no time is available at this point. Check again for blue smoke as the engine is revved. Do not be shy to ask the driver to rev it up well.

N.B. Be very careful when removing plug leads as the engine is running – it is easy to get quite a nasty electric shock. Wear rubber gloves if possible.

6) Check the water in the radiator by removing the cap (carefully, when hot). The questions to ask are:

a) Is there any water!

b) What colour is it? Clear Pink/Blue = Antifreeze. If you buy it, check the level is O.K. during the winter. Dark Brown/Black = oil: a problem. Light Brown = rust, probably, which is normal.

c) Is it warm? If it is, this indicates the cooling system is O.K. and the water pump operating. Cars can quite easily make it from their parking bay through an auction and back without a cooling system. You must check! Often if the radiator leaks vendors will enter a car without water in it. Fleet cars may more innocently have simply leaked dry. Now you can close the bonnet.

7) Open the boot and inspect the spare tyre. Check that the boot floor has not been replaced and that the light clusters are original to ensure the car has never had a rear-end shunt. Any ripples in the floor of the boot should put you off completely.

8) Get into the passenger seat. Ask the driver to depress the clutch and see that the gear stick engages all gears (and

reverse) smoothly. In the case of an automatic ask the driver to depress the foot brake and do the same test. Check the service history in the glove compartment, with an eye to the following:

a) Make sure it belongs to the car by checking the registration number in the front inside cover. It is easy to be tricked with false documentation.

b) Check that the mileage recorded does not make any jumps (indicating a new speedometer has been fitted) and that services were stamped, dated and carried out regularly. Be wary of a service history with all entries completed in the same pen – they have probably just been done!

9)   Ask the driver about the state of the clutch. He will probably be truthful. If the clutch is worn then the car will tend to lurch forward as it engages late. A new clutch fitted should be about £250. If the clutch has had it, the car will have an engine/transmission sound like an automatic.

10) Check the brake system by pumping the brake pedal three or four times until the pedal feels hard. Push on it and wait. If there are no leaks the pedal should not reach the floor at any point and, once pumped up, the pedal should not tend to depress when consistent pressure is applied. If there is a grinding noise when the brakes are applied then there may be one of three problems:

a) Rust in the drums/discs. This will wear off and simply develops through standing.

b) Pads are worn down or need replacing at about £25 per wheel.

c) Discs are warped or worn (unlikely if there is a full service history) caused by heavy braking and heat; will need replacing at up to £100 per wheel. Given time, one can check these easily through inspection posts on the hub, but the simplest test is to listen as the car draws to a halt.

Finally: Try everything electrical you can get your hands on, including stereo and electric windows.

If you have found time to carry out all these tests then I congratulate you! Nevertheless, they are simple but revealing tests which give you the opportunity to reduce the price you intend to offer or may even make you decide not to bid at all.

Checking under the bonnet for misalignment of wings and shock absorber struts etc. is a very important test. Although it isn't easy to be sure what you're looking for in a car that is basically O.K., it usually stands out proud on a problem car. Not only that but your initial overspray check should have alerted you to potential problems once under the bonnet! The reason it is so important to make this check is simply that damage that has been carefully hidden on the outside is generally much more obvious under the bonnet.

It is frightening how many people buy at auction without carrying out any of these tests. They simply bid on the shiniest example that comes along. With this in mind, if you have a chance to put even half of the above steps to use, you will be in a much better position than those around you to make a realistic judgement.

Remember: It is far more difficult to feel confident that what you are doing makes sense when you are dealing with a perfect specimen that gives the correct test results each time. Have faith, though. After all, this is what you are looking for, and the less than perfect specimen is easier to spot than you expect. Once you have uncovered your first accident repair your confidence will grow.

12   Bidding on a 'Not Sold' Car
After Sale

Often a car does not meet its reserve value, and few cars at auction are sold without reserve. If this is the case it remains 'not sold' and is usually, although not always, announced as such. The margin between the highest bid and the reserve may be as little as £50 in the case of a provisional on which the two interested parties could not agree, or as much as £1,000 where the auctioneer has never had a sensible bid or has never held one because the reserve is clearly crazy. In either situation there is one distinct advantage and two other potential advantages to be had over buying within the sale. There are also one or two disadvantages. We shall take each one in turn.

Advantages

1) The auctioneers are usually able to tell you the reserve price on any not sold car, as long as it has gone through auction at least once. This obviously gives you the edge that you did not have before and allows a period in which to mull over your budget. You may even be able to persuade the auctioneer to tell you what the best bid has been to date. If the bid was close to reserve he will no doubt tell you without any qualms, thus allowing you the security of knowing that the car is not vastly over-valued by its reserve price.

2) The car is obviously a bit of a thorn in the auctioneer's side, especially if he has persuaded a company to lower its reserve and still not managed to get the trader or party

involved to meet 'half way' by upping his or her bid. In this case, and usually in the case of any not sold company car, there is a good chance that you will be able to get hold of the keys once the yard staff, who will have to accompany you, have settled down. Now you have all the advantages of the forecourt and an opportunity to buy at near the trade prices. What is more, you still aren't being hounded by a salesperson.

3) The price you have been given is the new reserve. It is possible that you may be able to bid this down still further over the counter, but remember that where the reserve was nearly met by the trade on the day, there may well be good reason for the auctioneer to believe that he can achieve the money for his client at the next sale. Under the other circumstances – where the reserve is so high no bid has ever been held – you must conversely remember not to be 'taken to the cleaners' by offering what represents probably not far off retail money in order to clinch the deal. How do you know which is the case? Two things should be in your mind.

a)   How far did the bidding go on the car when it did not sell in the ring?

b)   What figure did you arrive at from your research and valuations (see Chapter 10)?

In reaching this valuation in your mind you will also be in a position to ask lots of questions and gauge the way in which they are being answered. Also bear in mind that there is a good to fair chance of the car remaining unsold until tomorrow.

4) There are many and various reasons other than price which may cause a car to remain unsold. One of these is easy to establish almost immediately: it might be that there are twenty other exactly similar vehicles in the sale, twelve of which have indeed been sold. In this case it is unlikely that the left-overs are of any lesser quality than those that were sold. It's simply a case of supply outstripping demand, particularly if all the colours are similar.

Disadvantages

1)   The other more sinister reason for a car remaining unsold

is that it is a complete 'Nail', i.e. 'wreck', and the trade will have spotted this at a distance. Result: not sold. Here is a golden opportunity for you to test at your leisure your ability to spot such a beast by following the section in this guide about condition. A word of warning: be extra cautious when bidding on entries that are not declared 'DIRECT' when they have been or are being avoided by trade.

2) Because the car is not sold you will be paying, by definition, the price to which the trade would not go, i.e. slightly over current estimations of trade price. You can guard against going any more than slightly over as discussed in Advantage 3 (above). But bear in mind that you are being given the opportunity to bid against a known reserve in your own time. This, coupled with the possible chance to get the keys and have a good long check around, might be worth the extra cost to you.

If you are in no doubt that the car in question was indeed one that was under offer but not sold, and if you watched the bid being accepted then you are in a still better position. You can tell whether the final bid was accepted from a private or trade source simply by virtue of the fact that traders rarely come forward to give a deposit. If, then, a trader's bid was £50 away and he walked off, there is a very good chance he has every intention of bidding the same or less next sale.

The motor trade has a long memory and will get incredibly stubborn over a maximum figure, almost as if they are trying to teach the vendor a lesson. The only other reason for them to leave a bid so close to a buy is that they have been back to the car, found out that there is something wrong with it, and are thus relieved to hear that they are being asked for more money – which affords them their only way out of the deal.

This need not worry you since the sort of problem the traders may have missed initially will have been one that you will have been onto from the outset. You don't believe me? At every sale there are a number of very 'cool' traders who may in previous years have been as vigilant as you or I, but who now have enough money to straighten any minor bodywork problems. They use that fact as an excuse not to even walk around the cars on which they are bidding. I have seen people bid on cars that are damaged all along the rostrum side, but look fine from where they are standing. Needless to say these are important bidders for the auction, and rather than let them lose face too embarrassingly, the auctioneer will often draw their attention to the pit into which they are about to fall.

Buying a 'not sold' car is, then, much easier and almost as financially rewarding. And as long as you remain vigilant and apply all the rules that you will learn in this book, there is no reason to believe that the act carries any more risk than buying from the forecourt.

If you are looking for a nearly new car the chances are that there will always be a number of cars not sold that can be made available to you. In this situation it is probably better overall to make a bid out of sale since the main reason for these remaining not sold is that of supply outstripping demand. This being the case, and bearing in mind that there is rarely much room for manoeuvre on their reserves, you may well enjoy the relaxed out-of-sale approach and see whether you can get the keys (see Chapter 13).

13   Buying Nearly New Cars at Auction

What defines a 'nearly new car'? There are a huge number of cars sold every year at auction that are so nearly new it is hard to see why anybody ever pays through the nose for the privilege of being the first name on the log book, for that is about as much as you get for your soon to be lost money when you buy new.

There seems little sense in the wholesale replacement of cars between four and six months old, but the car market depends upon manufacturer discounts and deals with the biggest fleet operators to keep registrations on a high. Whatever the complex reasoning behind it, the fact remains that it is possible to buy cars with as little as 600 miles on the clock, at very much trade rates, nearly every day at auction sites across the country. If this is the level of investment that you are wanting to make in your next car then this must be, in my opinion, the cheapest and safest deal you will ever get.

Nearly every car less than one year old is still covered by the manufacturer's warranty, as long as the car has been maintained properly and has never been declared an insurance total loss. The auctioneers often declare whether manufacturer's warranty still applies, but for complete peace of mind the best course of action is always to ask.

Given that the car is still covered by manufacturer's warranty, then a lot of your fears can be laid to rest. There are few warranties as good as manufacturer's and these cars represent the safest buy you will ever make short of a brand new vehicle. The main difference between new and nearly new is the amount of capital you need to invest and the rate of erosion of that capital once you do. A new car driven average distances (say 10,000 miles per year) will lose approximately 25% of its list price value within the first six months. Were the owner to have bought the same vehicle when it was six months old, then during the next six months he would lose only 12% of what he had paid for it. This then suggests that the loss of value for a new car within the first six months is running at more than twice the subsequent rate. There is next to no data to show what the auction price would be for cars, say, only three weeks old. Clearly, there are not enough such vehicles being sold to allow reasonable statistical analysis to be carried out. Nevertheless, the odd car of such recent vintage does sometimes appear in the form of a 'snatch back'. In my experience the trade rarely knows how to value these cars, and the few that emerge actually sell for similar reductions on list value to those that are six months old.

These figures, and the associated graph on page 10 are plain for all to see and must be the only incentive that the buyer (who has capital enough to be considering a newer car) needs. On top of this comes the plethora of advantages that this market brings with it.

The first bonus is, of course, that these cars are usually sold with manufacturer's warranty outstanding, which will not expire until their first birthday (i.e. the date of first registration). The warranty question is easily resolved, as we have said, by asking the office staff whether it applies or not.

The next batch of incentives is based on the fact that nearly new cars sent to auction often arrive in huge batches, leading to quite significant imbalance in model mix (i.e. there are often a large number of the same models).

If the auctioneer, and indeed his client, are especially unlucky they will even get loads of the same model in the exact same colour. All this leads to one thing, a lot of 'not solds'. The point of all this is that you, the buyer of nearly new vehicles, will not only be in a position to save a fortune by attending an auction of this type, but you will also be in the happy position of not having to buy within the sale. Furthermore, the way in which the reserves are often set is in your favour. Because of the volumes involved in this mass disposal of cars, the reserves are often presented to the auctioneers in terms of a list of prices which have set breaks at mileage intervals of around 6,000 miles. The reserve is usually closely adhered to in order to prevent under-sale of vehicles in off weeks or in situations of over-supply. With this in mind you can be fairly sure that if any of the models in which you are interested have sold, then you will be faced with a sensible price to pay.

How to Get the Best Out of Buying Nearly New

First, attend the sale and try to establish which models are actually selling and for how much. By keeping a note of the sale prices in your catalogue and comparing these to mileages you will be able to build up a picture of the 'price list' inside the auction office. You will soon recognize slight deviations from the rule as your list develops, and these are due to the occasional car having been reduced for various body repairs that may have been carried out. The evidence of the damage on which the vendor has made his reduction is just as available to you as it is to him. It is all drawn up by visual inspection of paintwork and overspray detailed by the vendor's inspectors on the condition report that is attached to the back of the entry form. It will be well worth your while to check the nearly new car as closely as you would a used one. Refer to the section dealing with condition, paying most attention to paintwork. It is up to you what you do with the information that you find on inspection. It could be used to ensure you are paying the least possible price, or it could be so extensive as to indicate major damage and send you off to examine the next car instead. Two things are worth noting at this stage. First, the quality of the repairs to bodywork on minor damage to these cars is usually quite good. Second, extensive damage, however well fixed, is best avoided. After all, there is always another day and another car.

If you can get the keys to the car (after the sale) so much the better. Look in particular for repairs to the boot floor (highlighted by irregularities in soundproofing felt, etc.) and to the inner wings under the bonnet (see Condition of Bodywork, page 69).

Use the guidelines and your common sense to seek out

major accident damage in this way and, if you can't find any, ask yourself: (a) Is there any to find? (b) if I can't find it how extensive could it have been, so does it really matter?

Remember, though, that once you have bought the car you are still governed by the auction regulations and that, although manufacturer's warranty adequately covers mechanical faults not caused by mis-use, there will be no recourse for bodywork.

Extra Cover or Extended Warranty

If you are someone who really feels strongly about being protected against the unforeseen, then it is often possible to buy extended warranty agreements on used cars less than one year old. If you are planning to buy a car on the strength of this, then please enquire of your main dealer about the current state of play. Some manufacturers will no longer provide the service, whilst others are only too keen to help as long as a full service history can be produced to prove proper maintenance. A last point on extended warranty: although it represents one of the most comprehensive warranties available, it does not come cheap (a year's cover is £300 to £500). Also, it will usually require that the service history is kept up-to-date which, although advisable on a car of this value, is also quite an expense to bear.

14 Checking Your Purchase

So you have done it. Your hand went up and, like it or not, you are the proud new owner of Lot X!

Please – don't immediately jump into the car, start it up and roar off at great speed. Whatever its age, your new purchase might well be missing a vital part or two, however carefully you have checked it out pre-auction!

You will probably have bought a car without trial and you will be aware by now that any major fault comes with the car as an added extra. Most likely there will be nothing terrible to discover, but that doesn't mean that there definitely will not be. Better to discover your problems at 5 mph than 50 mph! After all, this is your life you're dealing with.

Before you set off you must carry out a few simple checks, especially if you didn't get a chance to check the car over properly when it was coming through the auction hall:

1) Check your levels: Oil, Water, Brake Fluid. In each case you will find level indicators on the dip stick, radiator, expansion reservoir and brake fluid reservoir. If in doubt refer to the user manual.

Where the car is fitted with a non-pressurized cooling system, i.e. no expansion reservoir from the radiator, then remove the radiator cap (carefully if hot) and visually check that the level is within about ½ in. from the hole you are looking into.

These checks are most important, and if you are uncertain as to how to carry them out then you frankly should not be driving a car at all! So learn! Ask a member of the auction yard staff, or, if one isn't available, then ask a by-stander.

He or she probably will be in the trade and will usually assist.

If you have chosen a 'fully serviced straight off the road, genuine ex-fleet car', then no doubt all these levels will have been checked within the last few thousand miles and they will be O.K. – but do check them again!

If you haven't been so lucky, then you will thank yourself for these few minutes spent. Driving a car with no oil results in a seized engine very quickly; no water and overheating can buckle the head, etc.

2) Next, start the car and, leaving the bonnet open, check the following:

a) That there are no obvious leaks from the cooling system.

b) That the engine isn't 'knocking' – a clattering sound like stones in a bucket coming from the camshaft, either at the top or the bottom of the engine. If it is knocking badly you will know straight away. Don't mistake the general clatter as 'knocking'. Listen for a less regular pattern of loud clacks. 'Knocking' is caused by the camshaft and or the big end wearing, and is caused by the 'bouncing' of the valves in the case of camshaft wear on and off their cams. The big end bearing is a heavier knock. This comes from deep within the engine and heralds a complete strip down, if not a new engine.

If your car is making knocking sounds that are distinctly obvious then don't panic. First, ask a member of the auction staff whether there is any chance of obtaining the advice of their engineer, or anybody acquainted with the problem that you have. Unless you are a dab hand at motor mechanics then this person, whoever they may turn out to be, will advise you as to the imminence of the problem.

It is less than likely that you will have bought a car that won't get you home, but it is possible, and the amount of damage that can be caused by driving a car whose camshaft or big end is about to go is far worse than the damage to your pocket by sorting the problem before it reaches a climax.

The less checking you do before you bid the greater the chances of buying a 'nail'. Knocking is one of the bigger costs involved in buying the 'wrong' car. Rest assured that it only happens in cars that have covered a lot of miles – or been really very horribly treated. If your mileage check stacks up to a genuine low mileage car, then 'knocking' should not be one of your problems.

3) Turn the steering wheel, feel for any play. There should only be a little movement in the steering wheel before the front wheels themselves begin to move. If this play is excessive it may be worth having the car transported by the auction to the nearest tyre centre such as ATS to be checked before you drive.

The cost involved in correcting steering is not excessive, but steering itself is of paramount importance. Should there be little or no play, then you are probably safe to drive the car straight to ATS to have the steering checked anyway. It only takes a knock on the kerb to put your tracking off. A quick test now could save you a set of front tyres, and probably will. The cost of adjusting tracking is probably less than £20, and as often as not the test to see whether it is necessary is free. If a major fault in the tracking is brought out you may well have saved your life as well as your tyres!

4) Check that all your tyres are legal, using at best a tread gauge, at worst your judgement. You can have this checked again when you visit your tyre centre on the way home.

Never drive a car that is running on bald or illegal tyres. The results of a skid could be lethal, and the results of a conversation with an alert police officer will undoubtedly be very expensive. The auctioneers are under no compulsion to ensure your lot is legal to be driven on the road – you are. Check the Terms and Conditions.

5) You are now in a position to move the car.

Driving very steadily, in an area clear of other cars, check that the brakes work. Remember – do this test at low speed, and be aware that uneven wear on brake pads may cause the car to skew left or right. If you damage any vehicle on site you will be held responsible – so go steady.

6) Given that you are now happy with the safety of your car on the road, then you are ready to leave. Showing your 'pass-out' at the gate your destination should be: (a) local tyre Services; (b) local main agent for a service.

Servicing

Until you have had the car properly serviced, do not be tempted to 'see how it goes'. Be patient – stay alive! Even if you are, like me, a 'service-it-yourself' type, you must always take a car bought from auction for a full service.

Ask for a proper check to be made on all the moving parts. Explain to the service manager where the car has come from and why it is in for service. He may be able to offer you what is known as 'PDI' or pre-delivery inspection. It all depends on your pocket, but bear in mind that this is the point at which the car is to be declared safe for your personal use, and also that you have just saved a small fortune by buying from auction.

Service History

If your car has full service history to date, then think to the future. When you sell the car it will make a significant difference in its value if you sell with Full Service History. If the service history is already patchy, then the rule of thumb does not apply, but the general rule for production of a full service history is that you get nearly as much back for the vehicle as the servicing has cost you over the years – plus having the satisfaction of knowing that your car is O.K. whilst you are using it.

These days it is almost imperative that cars are properly serviced on a regular basis, a job best left to professional mechanics. Without the specialized training and all the magic gadgets of today's garages, the chances of you yourself successfully servicing your car (particularly if it's a luxury model) are pretty slight.

What Documentation to Keep

1) Invoice – proof of purchase contact point with the auction house.

It may also be worth your while asking the name of the person who served you and jotting it down on the invoice itself, especially in the case when payment was made in cash.

2) Top copy and lot number displayed in windscreen.

Where top copies are displayed then the information therein is binding and, should any problems materialize in the future with regard to the mileage, total loss declaration or any other mis-interpretation of your vehicle, then this document will be most important to your argument. It is also of use to convince prospective purchasers, or another auction hall, of the genuine nature of your claims.

3) Log book and MOT where appropriate.

If no log book is available and you wish to tax the vehicle immediately, then you may complete form V62 on application for one at any Post Office. You will thus require only the MOT (for vehicles over three years old) and insurance cover in accompaniment to your payment. In this case it is often worthwhile, but not deemed a necessity, to take along the auction invoice as proof of ownership.

Problems & Disputes – Who to Ask

The first port of call in every case should be the auction manager. If you are still not happy then the best method of approach is through Trading Standards. Contact your local Citizens' Advice Bureau and they will put you in touch with your local Trading Standards Officer.

Before you make contact collect all your information together, including terms and conditions of sale from the auction house. Consider your complaint and try to make some notes in order that you impart all the relevant facts to the officer you speak to, making your intentions clear. As long as you have a reasonable cause for concern the Trading Standards will investigate further and have access to all the information held by the auctioneer.

Should you discover that your problem has fallen on deaf ears, then you have probably been unlucky and there is no way out but to pay up and buy the vehicle in question. If this is the case, do not despair. You have two options:

1) Keep the car and get used to its ailment;
2) Sell it on.

Re-Sale of Unwanted Vehicle – Where to sell

Probably the best solution to selling a problem car is to put it back in the auction. If your case has raised a bit of a stink you may be able to persuade the auctioneers to offer you a reasonable rate of commission for re-sale as an incentive to keep you on their side as best they can! Should you re-sell through an auction then use the original top copy to work off and create a new entry form. Copy the details very carefully onto the new form.

Even though you have 'owned' the car, if you have not registered as the owner then there is no reason why you should not sell it as having had the same number of owners as was the case when you bought it.

The only thing you will not be able to duplicate from the original entry form is the statement 'Direct From', because the car has been in your hands.

Preparation for Re-sale

The car should be prepared as well as it possibly can for sale. Remember, people make a living from doing exactly this:

T-cut
  A slightly abrasive compound which removes layers of oxidized paint; can be used to polish out light scratching and gives an excellent shine to 'solid colours'. Do not over use 'T-cut' on lacquered finishes, i.e. metallic paint, because it is easy to cut through the lacquer to reveal the dull paint beneath.

Polish
  Every car looks better for a good polish, especially when it rains!

Back to Black, Cockpit cleaner etc.
  Try not to get carried away with this side of your preparation. The result tends to be greasy looking if overdone and stands out a mile as a 'private' entry.

Hoovering the carpet, seats etc.
  You can never spend too much time on a car's upholstery. VAXING is often the best method of getting really clean results, but test for colour-fastness on a small area before

anything is wetted!

Professionals in this field have been known to spend two or three days solid preparing a car for sale, removing seats, bumpers, headlights, trim, steering wheel, etc. to get rid of dust and dirt, creating that new car feeling – at a profit! They claim that the difference this extra valet makes is indeed worth the extra time.

Remember the tax implications of re-selling a car for more than you bought it (see Appendix 10), and don't get greedy. The best way to deal with any re-sale of an unwanted purchase is to set the reserve at only what the car owes you.

Do not expect to win other than to escape at a loss of only a day's work polishing. You may be in for a pleasant surprise, however. A case in point was an exceedingly irate lady with a Mini Metro that she had bought. Not able to reject the sale under our terms and conditions, I offered to re-sell it at a substantially reduced commission. She did not even polish the car and yet made £150 clear profit on an outlay of £750!

15   Step by Step Guide to Buying

1) Choose a number of suitable models, leaving final selection until the time of viewing.
2) Establish an idea of the retail value of your choices through tracking publications and newspaper ads.
3) Ring round the auctions to save time and trouble in finding your car. Ask for valuation at auction.
4) Check the terms and conditions of sale.
5) Check the auction house is an SMA member.
6) Check payment terms.
7) Select your vehicle from the following: Date Registered/ Mileage Warranty/Engine Size/Model Description/MOT/ Tax/Log Book/Total loss. Read statement on windscreen or ask staff for details.
a) Look for any extensive damage repairs by checking paintwork.
b) See that mileage numbers align neatly; check for wear to seat and wheel.
c) Check that service history is complete and applies to the vehicle it is in.
d) Is the car direct? How many owners has it got? Ask!
e) Check tyres for wear/remoulds, including spare.
f) Check inner wings, front facia and boot floor for repairs. Look for rippled metalwork and unconforming under-seal and damping matts.
g) Check for ripples in roof indicating twisted chassis. Major accident repairs must be evident (front or back) if these ripples occur.
8) Mechanical Checks:
a) Listen for knocking of camshaft or big end.

b) Check all fluid levels: oil, water, brake fluid.
c) Check oil filler cap for water (milky residue).
d) Check 'blow back' by covering oil fill hole with palm of hand.
e) Check exhaust emission when revving (blue indicates piston wear).
f) Check brake pedal for sponginess.
g) Check all electrical operations, including radio.
h) Check clutch (manual). Ask driver.

Mileage

CHECKING THAT A MILEAGE CLAIM STACKS UP AS GENUINE

1) Odometer should align sensibly:

a) $02987^{8}\,.^{7}_{8}$ – Genuine

b) $0_{2}9_{8}7^{8}\,.^{7}_{8}$ – Clocked?

The latter may look unlikely, and is probably a pretty bad job done by the clocking fraternity, but I have actually seen a car sold declared genuine 46,000 miles whose clock looked exactly like this.

2) Wear and tear on pedals etc.:

Often the professional villain will replace worn elements such as steering wheel, pedals, carpet etc. It is less likely that the driver's seat will have been replaced, but if it has been then it is even less probable that the entire set of seats has been changed. Check mismatch in colour of seats front and rear with special attention to the car whose driver's seat is the least worn or faded!

Should pedals, steering wheel etc. be extremely worn, then either the clocker is an amateur or there has been a genuine mistake made in the declaration – especially in the case of a direct company sale.

Check the steering rack for excessive wear by turning the wheel, which should be close to its original state, not shiny and smooth. There should not be a lot of play before the front wheels are turned in either direction.

The pedals should show slight wear commensurate with mileage e.g. any 20,000/30,000 mile car with brake pedal rubber worn through should be questioned.

At low mileage the driver's seat should still give support and the foam within feel firm.

Carpets and mats should not be worn through in the driver's foot well. All these checks and application of a modicum of common sense are perfectly valid, but there is no substitute for a full service history, direct fleet entry and proper investigation as to the vehicle source.

Chassis Numbers

The chassis number should always be checked on every car prior to purchase. Each number should match the next and also match the log book. Furthermore, they should never appear tampered with in any way. If in doubt, leave it!

POSITION
1) Most modern cars have their number stamped clearly into the shell on a chassis plate in the floor pan beside the driver's seat. All engines have an engine number on the block. Under the bonnet a manufacturer's plate riveted to the body has the chassis number, model details, etc.

Often the chassis plate is under a small flap in the carpet. This is always the case for a Ford. Metros have chassis numbers on the gutter at the back of the bonnet. Some Japanese cars have the number stamped directly onto a front suspension strut.

The older the car the more likely it is to have its chassis number hidden away. But whatever the case, the number should also appear on a plate riveted to the body.
2) The number stamped onto the manufacturer's plate, riveted in an area under the bonnet, should tally with the chassis number itself. Usually the plate is silver and easily spotted. But remember, the most important of the two is the chassis number, stamped deep and clear into the floor pan. To properly replace this there would need to be a removal of

the entire floor pan and re-stamping. This is expensive and, of course, not lightly undertaken by the average bodyshop. What usually happens when a car is criminally tampered with is that the old chassis plate is drilled out and replaced by lots of spot welding with a foreign lump of steel. Or it may be simply filed down and another number stamped over the top.

Both of these techniques are easy to see. To check if the number has been drilled out and replaced, simply look underneath the car for unconformities in underseal, or evidence of the spot welding itself. Filing down is obvious through streaks in the metal indicating the motion of the rasp, and the numbers punched are often not clear as a result of the past abrasion.

Spot welding is just that, and it appears as lots of metal blobs around the fitted sheet. Check underneath for new underseal or spots themselves.

Bibliography

A Handbook of Consumer Law
Which? Books National Federation of Consumers' Books
Consumers' Association
2 Marylebone Road
London NW1 4DX

The Sale of Goods (P.S. Atiyah)
Pitman Publishing
128 Longacre
London WC2 9AN

Halsbury's Laws of England (4th edition)
Volume 2, paragraphs 901 & 943
Volume 41, paragraphs 700 & 702
Volume 9, paragraph 366A

Butterworth & Co. Ltd
Borough Green
Sevenoaks
Kent TN15 8PH

(An extensive reference running into numerous volumes)

Passing the MOT (David Pollard)
Pass The MOT. How to pass the MOT first time and every time.
Veloce Publishing
Godmanstone
Dorset DT2 7AE

Some useful photographs and descriptions of condition advice, including the Ten Minute Guide which focuses on an MOT pass.

Top Gear Good Car Guide (Quentin Wilson)
BBC Books 1993
BBC Enterprises Ltd
Woodlands
80 Wood Lane
London W12 0TT

Useful guide to available models, making it particularly helpful for those in two minds as to what they are looking for. Also some useful tips on used car buying.

Haynes Manuals
Haynes Publishing
Sparkford
Nr Yeovil
Somerset BA22 7JJ

Model by model service and mechanical guides. These are the DIY bible for those who intend to service and repair their cars themselves. Very detailed in terms of the inspection time available at auction.

Buying a Second-Hand Car (Tony Bosworth)
Robert Hale Ltd
Clerkenwell House
Clerkenwell Green
London EC1R 0HT

Armed with a copy of this comprehensive guide to condition, the prospective buyer will have a far greater chance of spotting problems during the inspection prior to purchase, especially since this book picks out recurring and common faults on specific models.

APPENDIX 1

Glossary of Terms

Bids The offers received from the assembled buyers by the auctioneer during the sale. The bids are always nett of any VAT (commercial sales) or indemnity fees that may be applicable.

Buzz The atmosphere created by the auctioneer that gives a feeling of urgency and excitement. Attending a sale being run by a good auctioneer is the only way one can really understand what the term means.

Catalogue Sales Usually lots are sold at car auctions by driving the car into the auction hall. There are times, however, when a sale is carried out off catalogue. This means that the auctioneer will refer to lots in the order that they appear in the catalogue, even though they may be outside the auction hall or off-site altogether. In these cases a catalogue should be made available to the prospective purchasers, who should carefully examine the lots before the sale. Some nearly-new cars are sold off catalogue as well as being driven through. The catalogue in this case is a marketing tool to attract buyers chasing a specific model/colour.

Chassis No. or VIN This number is wholly unique to every car and forms the basis of all identification. It is stamped onto a solid part of the car's chassis so that it is not easily defaced without suspicion being aroused. The chassis number on any car *must* tie in with the log book exactly. If it does not, then something serious is amiss. *Always* check this correlation as soon as you receive the log book, as some auction companies stipulate a minimum period after receipt of the documentation for any complaints regarding title.

Chip A 'chip' off the price or a reduction in price, usually negotiated with the vendor when the buyer has found something lacking in the car and agrees to accept compensation. A chip will only be negotiated at times when the buyer has every right to rescind or cancel the sale according to the terms and conditions of the auction. Do not be pressured into accepting a chip if you are not satisfied. Reject the car and start again. Likewise, do not expect a chip if there is no case.

Depreciation Decline in value.

Direct The term used by auction companies across the UK to refer to a fleet car that is offered for sale by the company that has been using it, without any intermediary owners (i.e. a car that has been entered for sale by the fleet operator *directly* to the auction).

Entry Form The document on which the vendor enters all necessary details about himself and the vehicle, including the reserve. This form is drawn up by each auction company and serves as a legal document for their purposes and the basis on which all their business is carried out.

Ex-fleet A car or van that is being offered for sale through any third party (auction trader etc.) that has previously been used by a large company.

Ex-hackney Ex-hackney means that the car in question has previously been registered for use as a taxi. This generally implies that the car has had a hard life and the value reflects this.

Ex-Police These cars are easily recognized. They are white and have holes in the roof where lights etc. were attached. Although they usually have been 'round the clock' they are, never the less, well maintained. Their appearance and mileage are reflected in their perceived value.

Forecourt The area in front of a garage or vehicle sales office on which cars are offered for sale. Also called the pitch or showroom.

Full Service History A full service history is one that has been fully stamped by a main agent for the make of car, without any gaps and at the intervals set out by the service book. There are often occasions when a vehicle has been serviced slightly early or slightly late, but the extent of the deviation from the designated schedule must not be excessive in order for the history to be deemed 'full'. Beware false service history (i.e. one which has been fraudulently stamped by a third party). The only way to verify a service history is to telephone the dealer that stamped it.

Garagist Owner of a pitch or forecourt. Also trader/dealer/ main agent etc.

Gavel The auctioneer's hammer is known as a gavel.

Genuine A car that has not been touched up or presented in a better light than it deserves. This is a vehicle which has always been well maintained and looks as 'genuine' before it is valeted as after.

HPI A company specializing in holding information about a vehicle's history. It is their registration of a vehicle on their Vehicle Condition Alert Register which often defines the auction's determination of 'total loss'. They also hold information about finance agreements on vehicles (see Appendix 2).

Indemnity Auctions provide an indemnity system which is in effect a guarantee of clear title to any car bought through them. One has to contribute to the indemnity fund through an indemnity fee, payable on purchase (see Chapter 8).

List price The quoted cost of a new car before VAT and any special car tax or delivery fee etc. is applied. These days cars are usually displayed at the 'on the road' price, which includes all the associated extras but is fundamentally defined by the manufacturer's list price.

Log Book/V5/Vehicle Registration Document This is the document that is issued by the DVLA (Driver Vehicle Licencing Authority) that shows the name and address of the registered keeper of the vehicle, the date of first registration, and useful data on the make and model of the vehicle, which includes the chassis number and the registration number. Any vehicle bearing a registration number must also have a log book. The log book is a legal document and it is against the law to allow false or out-of-date information to be entered therein.

Lot Each vehicle entered has a lot number which is used throughout the selling process as a point of reference for that vehicle and should be unique to that particular vehicle. The lot number does not, unfortunately, always define when the vehicle is to be offered for sale in relation to the other lot numbers.

Main Agent/Dealer Garages holding a manufacturer's agency and thereby having the right to sell that manufacturer's cars new. These agencies are 'stand alone' businesses which do not belong to the manufacturer but are answerable to them to the extent that they may have their right to sell that manufacturer's cars withdrawn if they perform badly.

Nail Knacker/Dog Any such derogatory references are directed at a car that is deemed worthless for whatever reason. The quality of the comment depends upon the mouth that utters it. If a bidder loudly declares such derision, it may be that he hopes to put off his contestants. If the yard foreman says it, it may be that he genuinely has a grievance toward the car as it is he who has to see that all the cars are presented at the rostrum on time.

Manufacturer's Closed and Management Sales These sales are 'closed' to the public. The only people allowed to buy at a proper manufacturer's sale are the main agents that deal in that manufacturer's product. Usually the vehicles being sold are ex-management cars, well looked after and, more importantly, often fitted with a lot of optional extras. The main agent benefits from being able to buy these particularly nice nearly-new vehicles for retail, and the manufacturer enjoys two advantages. (1) He appeases the main agents. (2) He prevents the sale of these ex-management cars straight to the public, thus making them available only at retail prices which, accordingly, prevents a devaluation of his product at list price.

Manufacturer's Warranty The warranty that the makers of the vehicle give with every new vehicle they produce. The period and terms of the warranty vary from one manufacturer to another. When buying 'nearly new' it is very important to check that this sort of warranty still applies to the car you buy and that it is transferrable to you, the new owner.

Nearly new Cars and vans less than one year old and having less than 20,000 miles on the odometer. The age of a car is defined generally as the date of first registration.

Non-runner A loose definition covering any vehicle that cannot be driven into the auction hall. If the engine works the auctioneers will usually have the vehicle pushed through and started in front of the rostrum. They also will usually point out the problems that they are aware of but will not be held responsible for any that they miss.

Not Sold All the vehicles left over at the end of the sale that did not get bids close enough to or above their reserve price. These may be re-entered at a later date or returned to their owners.

Odometer The meter found on the speedometer, which records total mileage covered. This should not always be relied upon, and great care must be exercised in establishing the correct mileage.

Provisional A bid that is close to but under the reserve may be referred to the vendor for a decision. Thus the sale is 'provisional'.

Quick Knock Occasionally an unscrupulous auctioneer will bring the hammer down on a lot very quickly, thereby denying the other bidder the chance to bid again. There are limits to how long any auctioneer can wait for a bidder to make up his mind, but there are also times when a dubious employee may have reason to want a car sold to his partner in crime for less than it is really worth.

Reserve This is the figure set by the vendor (before any charges that may be levied by the auctioneers) that defines the absolute minimum that the vendor is willing to sell the vehicle for. The reserve is rarely disclosed to a prospective buyer before the sale and is usually applied to all vehicles less than ten years old, although the age rule varies between auctions.

Retail The price paid for a vehicle bought from any

forecourt. This price varies from forecourt to forecourt but is generally significantly more than the auction price.

Rostrum The raised platform on which the auctioneer and his/her assistant stand, affording them a good view of the crowd.

Total Loss Various definitions are quoted, but this effectively means that a vehicle has undergone major accident damage to the extent that it is deemed too expensive to have repaired by the insurance company covering it at the time. Generally a quotation for repairs running at over 50% of the current trade price of the vehicle will constitute a total loss.

Trade price The underlying value of the vehicle, usually defined by the auction price.

Trial or Warranty This term may be seen on an auction entry form. It indicates whether the vendor wishes to give a trial period at the end of the sale. This period usually lasts for one hour and gives the purchaser the opportunity to back out of a deal if a major mechanical defect is uncovered during the trial period that has not been disclosed on the entry form. The trial covers only the major mechanical elements and in no way represents a warranty in the true sense of the word in that it often expires one hour after the end of the sale, whether the buyer has taken advantage of it or not. It is not compulsory for any vendor to offer a trial but it is compulsory that he/she declare on the form whether a trial is to be offered or not. See Chapter 2.

Trotting The practice of raising the bidding by pretending there is another bidder (i.e. the auctioneer bids against a real bidder until the figure reached is high enough for him/her to offer it to the vendor).

Under the Hammer When the lot is sold during the auction for over reserve and the auctioneer drops his hammer to signify a sale. The hammer should only be dropped when a sale is made but beware that some auctioneers have a bad habit of banging it down for just about any reason, causing confusion in their attempt to build up an atmosphere of successful selling.

VAT See Appendix 10 to establish when VAT is payable on a lot.

Viewing The time when the general public can go onto the auction premises to look at the lots to be offered for sale.

Warranty Any sort of guarantee as to the quality of a vehicle, whether covering mechanics or bodywork. Most warranties are very specific.

APPENDIX 2

HPI

By putting a registration through its computerized database, HPI Autodata can tell instantly if that vehicle is recorded with them. If it is, they call it a 'hit'.

Marketing manager at HPI Niki Websper comments, 'the first quarter's HPI Autodata 'hit rates' show unequivocally that the public runs a one in three risk of buying a car that might give them cause for concern if they do not make an adequate check on that vehicle's history before purchase'.

When you buy from auction the indemnity fee you pay goes, in part, toward the purchase of HPI's service by the auctioneers. The auction thereby carries out an HPI check for you and also covers you for any future claims against title to the car (subject to varying terms and conditions of sale). If nothing else, the prospective buyer *must* read the section of the auction's terms and conditions that deals with the indemnity, since a proper auction indemnity is the best cover to title you will get.

Given that the terms are up to scratch, the auctioneers should guarantee clear title under the indemnity for at least five years. HPI cannot offer this level of guarantee. Indeed they point out that, 'The information held on HPI Autodata registers is supplied by police, by hire purchase rental and leasing companies, motor insurers, the DVLA, the Society of Motor Manufacturers and Traders, and the motor trade on a voluntary basis.' They go on to say, 'Whilst HPI Autodata takes reasonable care in recording and supplying information it cannot guarantee that the information is true, accurate or complete.'

Having highlighted this fact, I must also stress that it is in the interests of all those who supply HPI with their information that HPI should successfully provide the service that they offer. Although there are no guarantees this is the only service of its kind and is, in my opinion, invaluable.

HPI AUTODATA: THE SERVICE
Listed below, by kind permission of HPI Autodata, is the service they offer as of June 1994.

Vehicle Identity
Confirmation of the make, model, colour, engine size, transmission and fuel type for all vehicles registered after August 1986. This is based on the information recorded on the vehicle log book and originates from the initial vehicle registration documents.

Outstanding Finance
Comprising information on finance and leasing agreements provided by finance houses and leasing companies. If a registration number checked on HPI Autodata is on the Outstanding Finance Register, the enquirer will be given details of the type and date of the outstanding finance agreement and be encouraged to return to the vendor to obtain proof that the agreement had been paid off.

Condition Alert
Comprising information from members of the Association of British Insurers on major damage related insurance claims, where the insurance company handling the claim has decided to pay the owner the value of the car rather than pay for repairs. If a registration number is on the Condition Alert Register, the HPI Autodata enquirer is provided with the date of the claim and encouraged to have the car examined by a qualified person to ensure that it is roadworthy before purchase.

Stolen Vehicles
Featuring information on vehicles reported as stolen by the

police. If a registration number being checked is shown on the Stolen Vehicle Register, HPI Autodata will check the current circumstances of the registration with the police and provide the enquirer with these details. Callers will be advised not to proceed with the purchase until they are sure the person selling the vehicle has the right to do so.

Security Watch

Motor dealers, fleet and rental operators, finance houses, insurers and the police all use the HPI Security Watch to 'highlight' cars considered to be at 'high risk' from theft or fraud. The HPI Autodata response to a 'hit' on Security Watch will be to immediately contact the registering party, and advise the enquirer not to proceed further with the purchase until the details have been clarified further by HPI Autodata.

Plate Transfer

Features information from the DVLA to alert enquirers to vehicles which have undergone at least one registration plate transfer since April 1990. This provides the enquirer with the opportunity to discuss the matter further with the vendor, or to request HPI Autodata to investigate the situation on his behalf.

The information is supplied to HPI Autodata by the DVLA, the Society of Motor Manufacturers and Traders (SMMT), the finance and leasing industry, motor dealers and auctioneers, insurers, rental companies, the police and local government bodies. If any of the information suppliers have told HPI Autodata about a car, they can tell the public.

If you are considering buying a car privately or through an auction that, for whatever reason, does not offer an indemnity scheme, then I strongly advise that the HPI Autodata service be taken up. This is a relatively new service in that it used to be available only to account holders within the trade i.e. dealers, auctioneers, traders etc. Now that HPI have extended their service to the public, you should make use of it.

At the time of publishing HPI advise that: The HPI

Autodata hotline is open from 8.00 a.m. to 8.00 p.m., Monday to Saturday, and from 10.00 a.m. to 5.00 p.m. on Sundays. The service costs £15 per enquiry (including VAT), which gives access to all registers. Credit card payment (Access, Visa or Mastercard) will be accepted for telephone enquiries on 0722 422422. Cheque or postal order payment will be accepted for enquiries made by post.

Automobile Association
Vehicle Inspections

The AA offer a comprehensive inspection service at two levels: The 'mobile inspection' and the 'elite inspection'. If you are buying at auction only the mobile inspection will really be practical, and anybody requiring this service to be carried out prior to purchase must obtain the auction manager's permission before arranging it in order that keys may be made available.

It is, of course, possible that your request to carry out such detailed examination prior to the sale will be turned down. This may be the case for a variety of reasons, but it is more likely to be an administrative problem than any real worry of what the inspection will reveal.

The AA's elite inspection may well be worth considering immediately following purchase in order that any claim on the indemnity for 'total loss' can be raised as soon as possible.

It is worth remembering that the inspection service now offers an HPI check at no extra charge. This makes the service indispensable for anybody who buys either privately or from a forecourt.

AA Commercial Services provides the following description of its inspection procedures:

VEHICLE INSPECTIONS – PROFILE
An AA Vehicle Inspection provides a thorough and

independent mechanical check for any motorist, AA member or non-member, who wants to be sure the car they wish to buy is in a safe and sound condition and provides value for money.

The AA provides two services: the Mobile inspection and the Elite inspection.

The Mobile inspection is visual and external, without dismantling any part of the car, and checks more than 150 items, including: bodywork, cooling system, fuel system, engine, electrics, wheels, tyres, steering, suspension, underbody, exhaust system, clutch, gearbox, final drive and braking system. The AA engineer will also give the vehicle a road test.

After the inspection, the customer receives a comprehensive five-page written report giving all the information needed to make a decision on buying that specific vehicle. If required, an AA engineer can discuss any necessary repairs with the vendor and also provide a valuation of the car.

Elite inspections are carried out in virtually laboratory conditions at Autolign test centres. As well as covering all aspects of the mobile inspection, Elite uses computerized diagnostic equipment to detect faults in sophisticated auto systems, such as ABS and 4WD braking and engine management systems. Emissions testing reveals problems in engine and catalytic converter performance.

All AA engineers are ex-motor trade and motor industry, all qualified through the Institute of Road Transport Engineers or the Institute of Motor Industry. The AA has 100 vehicle inspectors covering the UK with an average of 15 years' professional experience of vehicle inspections, all regularly briefed with the latest information about auto engineering and motoring developments.

AA vehicle inspections can be booked by phoning 0345 500610.

MOBILE VEHICLE INSPECTION PRICES*

Group	Examples	AA Mem. Fee	Non-Mem. Fee
1	Rover Metro Ford Fiesta Vauxhall Nova	£99	£117
2	Ford Escort Rover 214 Vauxhall Astra & Cavalier	£110	£130
3	Vauxhall Carlton Rover 820 Renault 19	£132	£155
4	Range Rover Saab 9000 Volvo 960	£176	£207
5	BMW 7-series Rolls Royce Jaguar XJS/V12	£248	£293

ELITE VEHICLE INSPECTION FEES*

Group	AA Mem. Fee	Non-Mem. Fee
1, 2, 3	£158	£186
4	£202	£238
5	£285	£337

* All prices are inclusive of VAT and are correct as of June 1994.

Car Value Guides

There are many guides on the market today, and most are readily available to the general public in the major newsagents. Unfortunately, the best guides are the trade ones, of which there are two: *Glass's Car Price Guide* and *CAP Guide to Car Values*. I say unfortunately because neither is available outside the motor trade and circulation is strictly controlled.

Of the more readily available guides the choice and preference is largely a personal one. There is one very important thing to remember with any price guide: *it is only a guide*. Don't fall into the trap of believing everything you see in print. Don't assume that the guide can accurately represent the car market at any given time over the next month. Don't even assume that the prices listed are correct. Personally, I find *Parker's Guide* the easiest to reconcile with the actual market fluctuations, but take one or two to a sale and see how closely you can predict the selling price of each lot.

Useful guides include *Parker's Used, New and Trade Car Price Guide, The Motor Trade Guide to New and Used Cars* and *Car Trade Used Car Prices*. Don't forget that the trade magazines often publish a price guide as part of the editorial or as a supplement, and these can be very good. I was particularly impressed by that of *What Car* from May 1994.

APPENDIX 5

Useful Contacts

Organizations	Telephone Numbers
AA Vehicle Inspections	0345 500610
AA Insurance Services	0222 239999
	or locally in Yellow Pages
Eagle Star Direct (Motor quote)	0800 770600
Churchill Insurance	0800 200300
Direct Line Insurance	061 839 2468
RAC Insurance	0800 678000

(Before you bid always ensure that premiums are sensible for the car you intend to buy.)

DVLA (Swansea)	0792 772134
Trading Standards	Under local County Council or through local Citizens' Advice Bureau
HPI Autodata	0722 422422 (8 a.m. – 8 p.m.) Mon.–Sat. (10 a.m. – 5 p.m.) Sun.
Society of Motor Auctions	0645 502977

Auction Houses

ADT Auctions	21 Sites Nationwide
	0428 607440
Central Motor Auctions	7 Sites Nationwide
	0532 820707
National Car Auctions	6 Sites in England
	0206 250230
The Auction Consortium:	5 Independent Sales
Schotts (Strathclyde)	0501 823337
Westbury (Wiltshire)	0373 827777
Chelmsford (Essex)	0245 450700
Prees Heath (Shropshire)	0948 663166
Tamar (Cornwall)	0752 841444
Independent Car Auctions:	2 Sites
Bristol	0272 555141
Rotherham	0709 378989

All the auctions listed here are members of the Society of Motor Auctions at the time of writing. There are many other such auctions, too numerous to list individually.

APPENDIX 6

Schematic Diagram of an Auction House

[Note: Counter between entry office and general office is often split into separate sections.]

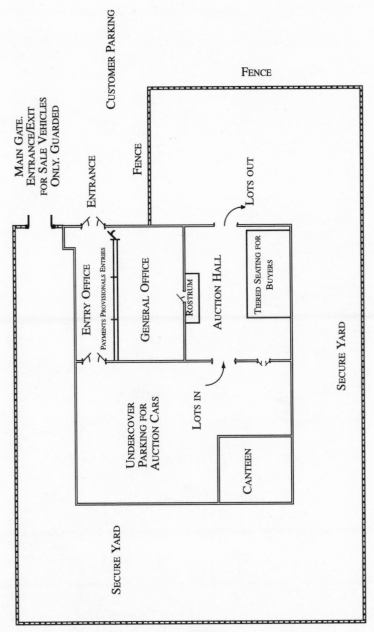

APPENDIX 7

Auctions and the Sale of Goods Act (1979)

When one buys or sells at auction it is often said that the Sale of Goods Act 'does not apply'. To an extent this comment is true, but it is not as simple as that nor as wide ranging.

The Sale of Goods Act (1979) refers directly to the auctions and their procedures. Indeed details including bidding procedures and reserves are carefully considered and specified under the rules. In fact the implication that there is no control under the act is misleading. To establish the extent of any exemption or restrictions applied to auctions, one must look at the contractual agreement made at the point of sale and defined by the terms and conditions of business of the auctioneers.

It is these terms and conditions that are governed by the Sale of Goods Act, as they are for any business. The difference between the auction and most other selling situations is that the auction is defined by section 12.2 of the 1977 act as specifically and categorically excluded from being a 'consumer sale'. This exclusion has a dramatic effect on the Unfair Contract Terms Act (1977), which exists to prevent suppliers from limiting or avoiding liability for their products by including conditions within their terms and conditions of business that are of an exclusory nature.

The Unfair Contract Terms Act defines a set of statutory restrictions on any exclusory term, i.e. it governs what may or may not be said within a supplier's terms to restrict that supplier's liability to the buyer. The supplier may not restrict:

1) Liability for selling any item on which there is not free title, i.e. no seller can exclude liability for selling something that is not free from incumbrance by reference to any contract term (the terms and conditions).

2) Liability for providing goods that do not match the quality of their description or that of the sample given or goods not suitable in fitness or quality for any given purpose by any contract term as to a buyer acting in a consumer sale.

Here lies the big difference.

Because auctions cannot be included as consumer sales, there is no restriction on the auctioneers to quote within their terms and conditions an avoidance of liability for part 2 of the Unfair Contract Terms Act.

This means that there may be terms within an auctioneer's terms and conditions that contract both the auctioneers and the sellers out of any liability for the goods on sale being of merchantable quality, as long as those terms are 'reasonable'. This is a requirement of the Unfair Contract Terms Act which states that where a non-consumer sale is affected the terms involved may be subject to the 'test of reasonableness'.

THE TEST OF REASONABLENESS

To establish whether a particular term meets this test, the following is taken into consideration:

1) The opportunity available for the buyer to purchase the goods elsewhere.

2) Whether the term itself could have been avoided by going elsewhere.

3) Whether the customer knew or ought reasonably to have known that the term existed.

4) Whether, if the term is restricting liability from some condition (often a time factor at auction), that condition could reasonably be complied with at the time of contract.

To clinch the auctioneer's right to contract out of any liability with regard to condition of any car sold, there is a statement that says that it is necessary for the auctioneers to communicate to the bidders any term that will have this exclusory effect. This may be done by notice, i.e. displaying the terms and conditions in the auction hall.

With regard to the test of reasonableness cited above, the auction house can argue as follows:
1) The consumer can always buy from the trade or main agents. The auctions have not got the monopoly on cars and, because the term can be avoided at a dealership, then (2) is also quashed, I would suggest. As for (3), the terms need only be displayed. In addition, the auctioneer and his/her staff are at pains to keep reminding the buyer to read the terms and conditions. Part (4) covers the demand for payment within a reasonable time scale. There is, however, a last clause in the buyer's favour:

EXCLUSION CLAUSES RENDERED VOID OR UNREASONABLE
If misrepresentation of a chattel is made by the seller before the contract was made, then there cannot be any exclusion of liability by any contract term nor any restricting clause on any course of remedy open to the buyer because of such misrepresentation. This stands except where a court or arbitrator considers the term or clause acceptable under the circumstances of the particular contract.

IN SUMMARY
As far as auctions are concerned, from the buyer's point of view the law is the same as for any sale, other than the fact that there is no liability on the part of the seller or auctioneers to sell an item deemed to be in a condition fit for its given purpose nor to provide any guarantee of the quality of the items sold. According to the law the auctioneer is not, however, in a position different than any other salesman in terms of giving a misrepresentation. But bear in mind that auctions do indeed contract out of this situation by stating that no one in their employ has the authority to pass comment on the quality or condition of any lot. Reflecting on the 'void or unreasonable' extract above, this seems a moot point, but it is possible that a judge might consider such a clause acceptable given the circumstances of the auctioneers employing such huge staff.
   The motto of the story is:
1) *Check* the car before you bid.

2) *Ignore* most of what is said about its condition, unless a very *specific* statement is made. Sometimes a defect will be highlighted to prevent later argument. Don't be misled into thinking this is a ploy to dampen the bidding. It is probably the truth.

APPENDIX 8

The Ex-Hackney, Private Hire
and Police Vehicles

WHY AVOID THESE CARS?

These vehicles are always high mileage and have had very heavy use. Police cars stay out on the road day and night, as do some taxi cabs. High mileage these days is not the issue it was fifteen years ago, but in these cases the mileages are exceptional and, what is worse, it represents a lot of stopping and starting which puts strain on every mechanical part of a car. In addition, the interiors are usually tatty and worn.

Nevertheless, these cars get sold, and when they are sold direct from the taxi firm or police authority there is indeed no real need to avoid them. After all, they will have been well maintained and, even more important, they will sell for prices that reflect their condition. The problem only arises when these cars return to the auction circuit in a new guise. Re-vamped, they can be made to look quite smart and thus sell (against most auction regulations) at considerably more than they are worth. Sometimes the work done is so good it is not easy to spot, but more often it is done quickly and cheaply to maximize the gain. In this case the following points will help the prospective buyers to spot a problem (especially in conjunction with the checks previously discussed).

SPOTTING AN EX-HACKNEY OR POLICE CAR IN
DISGUISE

The next time you are passing one, have a look at a taxi or
police vehicle that is still in service. This will enable you to
see the kinds of fittings employed locally and will help you to
pick out the disguised car later on.

If you're suspicious that a car may be ex-taxi or police,
look at the paintwork. This is the key to all problem cars. A
full respray (detected by overspray as discussed in Chapter
11) should arouse instant suspicion.

A full respray is common on disguised taxis or police cars
for the following reasons:

1) Transfers are removed from the bodywork (police
colours and stripes, taxi logos, etc.), damaging original
paintwork.

2) Holes must be filled and painted. (Holes are made in the
roof or boot of police cars to attach aerials and flashing
lights, or to attach illuminated signs and aerials on some
taxis.)

3) To cover two-tone paintwork on taxis, as specified by a
local council.

4) To disguise panel damage. These cars are prone to the
odd dent.

Look at the line of the roof to see whether there are any
unconformities or rippled areas that might indicate filler –
specifically, in the case of a police car, some 4–16 inches
(depending on the car) behind the windscreen. This patch
becomes obvious when sunlight is seen reflected off the roof
in a distorted fashion. Aerial holes can be checked for in the
same way on the roof, boot and wings. These are less
common with the modern use of magnetic aerials, but they
can still provide a clue.

Look at the bumpers. These are often used by police and
taxis alike as a platform on which to mount things. Light
arrays are common on police cars, as are the obligatory taxi
license plates. Look for holes left by self-tapping screws.
More recently other means of attachment have included
straps (which usually leave scratches or at least an area of
less faded paint/colour) and velcro pads (which leave,
occasionally, a glue deposit). Police cars often have lights

fitted to the front grill. Look for associated damage here – holes for wires, screw holes etc.

The outside of a car is easier to cover than the interior so look inside for:

1) Two-way radio mounts – Often under the dash beside the driver or in the glove compartment. Again, look for four holes made by small self-tapping screws.

2) Handset mounts – Try not to confuse these with very similar marks left by a car phone on a reputable fleet car. A small square or oblong bracket will have been held in place on the dash by four screws within reach of the driver.

3) Taxi meters – All taxis have a meter which will have been secured within sight of the customer, commonly in the glove compartment or on top of the dash. Look not only for screw holes but also wiring holes to supply the power.

4) General wear – See chapter 11. Look for clocking, replaced seats, carpets, foot pedals, steering wheel, etc.

5) Chassis No. – Check that it is not tampered with and note it down.

Documentation

1) Check that the chassis number tallies *exactly* with that in the log book.

2) How many owners? – If this is a taxi or police car it will almost definitely have three. You will see that these three may well have owned the car as follows. Number one (no longer listed in the log book) had it three to four years. Number two only kept it four or five months, and number three just bought it.

The three-owner routine

If you ever find a car that shows a record of keepers like that cited above, then you should immediately be suspicious of who the first owner was. This sudden turnover of owners is often used to dislodge the name of the first owner, which was probably a police authority or taxi firm.

Summary

1) Paint – Do not accept extensive paintwork on modern cars.

2) Unconformities – Where the line of the body doesn't run true, there has probably been filler.

3) Screw holes – Inside or outside the car, all taxis and police cars have had something fitted that will need holes drilling to accommodate it.

4) DIY Sun-roofs – These are sometimes a simple way of overcoming the problem of holes in the roof.

5) Wiring holes (generally the most difficult aspect to disguise and thus the easiest to spot) – Be wary not to confuse this with an innocent car phone. Police cars often show signs of the head lining being damaged where wires ran. Taxis often have holes in the back of a glove compartment through which wire ran.

One Last Point: Police cars are usually white, and taxis are usually diesels. BUY DIRECT FLEET and avoid the problem.

APPENDIX 9

The Driver and Vehicle Licensing Agency (DVLA)

The DVLA not only carry out the important function of registering vehicles and driver information but they can be of more assistance than most car buyers realize in terms of sharing some of that information to help in the fight against crime.

General enquiries should be made to Customer Enquiries (Vehicles) DVLC, Swansea on telephone number 0792 772134 between 8.15 a.m. and 4.30 p.m., Monday to Friday.

A dealer checkline is also available on which important data can be checked against a given registration number, make and model, including dates of first registration, year of manufacture, engine capacity etc. This service is of particular value in checking details in the absence of the log book and obviously helps to prevent misdescription. In some cases it also highlights a possible ringed vehicle where model changes can be pinpointed to the year of manufacture. The service used to be free of charge but is now only available on a premium rate number: 0839 858585.

MOT Checks

Another very useful service is provided by the Vehicle Inspectorate at Swansea, but it seems it is rarely taken advantage of. MOT test certificates are greatly sought after by thieves. They are essential to any car of more than three years of age and often represent a large outlay in terms of repairs to be obtained through legal channels. There has thus developed a black market for these valuable documents. If one is uncertain of the certificate presented with any car bought then it is imperative that it be checked out. Not only is it against the law to run a vehicle without a current MOT certificate but some thought must be levelled at the reasons behind any car being sold with a stolen or forged one if only from the point of view of its value. The Vehicle Inspectorate keep records of all stolen certificate numbers as reported by the MOT station which has lost them. By telephoning them and quoting data from the certificate that you hold they are able to confirm where and when it was issued if it is genuine.

The telephone number for this service is: 0792 454241.

APPENDIX 10

VAT

Generally VAT is not applicable to used cars or any other used vehicle with seats and windows behind the driver's seat, given that there are less than twelve seats in all.

VAT REGULATIONS
(Reproduced with the kind permission of Glass's Guide Services Ltd from their Guide to Car Values.

Definition of a car
For tax purposes a car must meet the following criteria:
a) Have side windows behind the driver's seat.
b) Be capable of carrying more than one but less than twelve persons.

First Disposal of tax-paid New Cars
The first disposal of a new car on which VAT was non-deductable when acquired new is now free of VAT provided the sale price does not exceed the original cost.

VAT New Cars
Is levied on the sale price. Is payable in full and not reclaimable. In short there is no VAT on used cars but there is VAT on vans. Where VAT is due it is levied by the auctioneers on the selling price.

Buying and Selling Used Cars and VAT
1) VAT is levied on the margin defined as the difference between the actual buying and selling prices.

2) The cash received for an unexpired vehicle licence must be deducted from the price paid to establish the buying price for VAT purposes.

3) No relief is allowed for expenditure on any car before re-sale.

4) No VAT credit is granted if the selling price is less than the buying price.

5) All used car prices are tax-inclusive and no mention of VAT due is disclosed on invoices.

6) Traders are required to maintain for each individual car deal:

a)   A purchase book
b)   A sale invoice
c)   A stock book.

For further reference:

Custom and Excise Notices
No. 700 – General Guide to VAT
No. 702 – VAT on Imports
No. 705 – VAT on Personal Export of New Motor Vehicles
No. 711 – VAT on Used Cars

Should you be inclined to begin 'trading' then it is imperative that these VAT requirements are respected and clearly shown in your accounts.

Beware of imported vehicles on which Import Tax is still due. This will always be declared or announced at auction when it is deemed payable. Make sure you spot the declaration – the tax involved in import/export is considerable. It is however rare that vehicles bought at auction on mainland Britain are still due import tax, and there will be a good deal of warning made of this if it arises.